Creating a Coaching Culture

Developing a Coaching
Strategy for Your Organization

Coaching in Practice series

The aim of this series is to help coaching professionals gain a broader understanding of the challenges and issues they face in coaching, enabling them to make the leap from being a 'good-enough' coach to an outstanding one. This series is an essential aid for both the novice coach eager to learn how to grow a coaching practice, and the more experienced coach looking for new knowledge and strategies. Combining theory with practice, it provides a comprehensive guide to becoming successful in this rapidly expanding profession.

Published and forthcoming titles:

Bluckert: *Psychological Dimensions to Executive Coaching*
Brown & Brown: *Neuropsychology for Coaches: Understanding the Basics*
Driver: *Coaching Positively: Lessons for Coaches from Positive Psychology*
Hay: *Reflective Practice and Supervision for Coaches*
Hayes: *NLP Coaching*
Rogers: *Developing a Coaching Business*
Sandler: *Executive Coaching: A Psychodynamic Approach*
Vaughan Smith: *Therapist into Coach*
Wildflower: *The Hidden History of Coaching*

Creating a Coaching Culture

Developing a Coaching Strategy for Your Organization

Peter Hawkins

McGraw Hill
Open University Press

Open University Press
McGraw-Hill Education
McGraw-Hill House
Shoppenhangers Road
Maidenhead
Berkshire
England
SL6 2QL

email: enquiries@openup.co.uk
world wide web: www.openup.co.uk

and Two Penn Plaza, New York, NY 10121-2289, USA

First published 2012

Copyright © Peter Hawkins, 2012

All rights reserved. Except for the quotation of short passages for the purpose of criticism and review, no part of this publication may be reproduced, stored in a retrieval system, or transmitted, in any form or by any means, electronic, mechanical, photocopying, recording or otherwise, without the prior written permission of the publisher or a licence from the Copyright Licensing Agency Limited. Details of such licences (for reprographic reproduction) may be obtained from the Copyright Licensing Agency Ltd of Saffron House, 6-10 Kirby Street, London EC1N 8TS.

A catalogue record of this book is available from the British Library

ISBN-13: 978-0-33-523895-8 (pb)
ISBN-10: 0-33-523895-5 (pb)
eISBN: 978-0-33-523897-2

Library of Congress Cataloging-in-Publication Data
CIP data applied for

Typesetting and e-book compilations by
RefineCatch Limited, Bungay, Suffolk
Printed and bound by CPI Group (UK) Ltd, Croydon, CR0 4YY

Fictitious names of companies, products, people, characters and/or data that may be used herein (in case studies or in examples) are not intended to represent any real individual, company, product or event.

The **McGraw·Hill** Companies

Contents

Series Editor's Foreword	viii
Acknowledgements	ix
Coaching Strategy Case Studies	xi
Introduction: Coaching at a crossroads – the challenge for chief executives, HR directors, heads of coaching, internal and external coaches, managers, coach trainers, and researchers	1
1 Setting the context: the growth of coaching and the challenges it now faces	11
PART 1: THE FOUNDATIONAL PILLARS	**19**
2 What is a coaching culture? The key ingredients	21
3 Creating a coaching strategy and aligning it to the wider organizational culture change	33
PART 2: THE SEVEN STEPS	**45**
4 Step 1: Developing an effective panel of external coaches	47
5 Step 2: Developing the internal coaching and mentoring capacity	60
6 Step 3: The organization's leaders actively support coaching endeavours and align these endeavours to the organizational culture change	79
7 Step 4: Coaching moves beyond individual formal sessions to team coaching and organizational learning	89
8 Step 5: Coaching becomes embedded in the HR and performance management processes of the organization	104

| 9 | Step 6: Coaching becomes the predominant style for managing throughout the organization | 114 |
| 10 | Step 7: Coaching becomes how an organization does business with all its stakeholders | 125 |

PART 3: INTEGRATION AND DEPTH — 137

11	How to get all the elements working together and aligned to the 'relational value chain'	139
12	Expanding the depth and improving the quality of coaching activities: supervision and continuous personal and professional development	152
13	Evaluation, research, and the return on investment from creating a coaching culture	160
14	Conclusion: the challenges going forward	175

| Bibliography | 183 |
| Index | 193 |

Dedication

To all those who have been working so hard to create coaching cultures within organizations, both those mentioned in the book and the many others known and unknown.

Quotes

To plant a tree is to leave a legacy. To create a garden is to change the ecology. Yet the garden must always leave space for wilderness to work its own magic.

What can coaching uniquely do that the world of tomorrow needs?

Series Editor's Foreword

As coaching has taken hold in organizations it has become clear that this leaves a big question unanswered: individual coaching is great, but how can we deliver its benefits to the whole organization?

In this much-needed title, Peter Hawkins gives a thoughtful, practical answer to the whole question of how you create a 'coaching culture'. It is certainly not just about 'doing a lot of coaching'. That it is a much more complex question than it first appears will be obvious when you read the book. You can only create a 'coaching culture' when coaching is committed to and properly understood at the most senior levels, when coaching is embedded into the organization's strategy and permeates all its systems and relationships, including those with customers and suppliers – a huge undertaking.

Peter is one of the few people worldwide to have first-hand experience and evidence to offer, and what he has to say goes beyond wishful thinking or theory. There are valuable lessons here whether you are a coach yourself, an organization consultant, a HR professional or a chief executive. It will answer such questions as: how would we know a coaching culture if we had it? Who needs to be persuaded of the benefits? How do we calculate the return on investment?

I commend this book to you as an insightful, clear and readable guide to what is inevitably a challenging but achievable journey for any organization.

Jenny Rogers
Series Editor

Acknowledgements

I would like first to thank all those people who have contributed to making this book possible.

Much of the material on which this book is based has been developed over the last thirty years or more in work helping organizations transform their organizational culture and introduce coaching activity. However, a great deal has emerged from my research over the last four years in many interviews and conversations with those responsible for coaching in a wide variety of organizations. Many of these hard-working coach pioneers have been very generous with their time and in writing some of the case studies that appear in this book. They are listed on the following pages.

I would also like to thank all those I have coached, mentored, consulted to, supervised, and trained. They have been my best and constant teachers in continuing to develop the craft, and continue to provide me with fresh challenges and challenging and encouraging feedback

The thinking in this book builds crucially on the work pioneered and written with my colleagues at Bath Consultancy Group (www.bathconsultancygroup.com) over the last twenty-five years. My colleagues in BCG have brought great quality of challenge and support to my thinking, writing, and practice in understanding organizational culture and how to work with organizations to develop it and how to support and develop coaching cultures. In particular, I would like to thank: Nick Smith for co-writing with me *Coaching, Mentoring, and Organizational Consultancy: Supervision and Development*, and letting me draw liberally from it in this book; Gil Schwenk, who along with Nick and myself has developed our joint work in coaching supervision; John Leary Joyce of the Academy of Executive Coaching, who has been a great colleague in devising together the first ever UK certificate programme in Team Coaching; and Dr. Patricia Bossons at Henley Business School. Each of them also commented on parts of the text, as did Marianne Tracy in New York and Peter Binns in Devon.

Malcolm Parlett and Judy Ryde have been great friends and colleagues on writing weeks, and my other colleagues at the Western Academy (Peter Reason, the late John Crook, and Peter Tatham) and Centre for Supervision and Team Development (Robin Shohet and Joan Wilmot) continue to challenge, support, and inspire me.

In preparing the text, I have had enormous support from my personal assistant Fiona Benton.

Finally, I would once more like to thank my wife and partner Judy Ryde for her love, patience, colleagueship, support, and for reading and correcting the text several times.

Peter Hawkins
Professor of Leadership, Henley Business School
President of the Association of Professional Executive
Coaching and Supervision
Emeritus Chairman, Bath Consultancy Group
Chairman, Renewal Associates

Coaching Strategy Case Studies

In writing this book I had a great deal of help from HR directors, coach managers, coaches, and coach trainers in many different companies who shared their particular journeys on a route to establishing a coaching culture. I am indebted to them for their time and openness and without their contribution this book would have lacked the richness of their stories. I have not been able to include case studies from all those who I talked with, but their experience has informed many of the recommendations in the book.

BBC – Liz Macann, Head of Coaching
Clutterbuck Associates – Liz Dimmock, Managing Partner
Department of Work and Pensions UK – Caron Twining, Principal Psychologist, Leadership and Management Development Team
Department of Health UK – Barbara Moyes
East Suffolk Health Authority – Dr. Penny Newman and Dr. Andrew McDowell
Electricity Supply Board Ireland – Paddy Stapleton, Senior Executive Coach
Ernst and Young – Nicki Hickson and Ian Paterson
Foreign and Commonwealth Office – Pamela Major and Karen Roskilly
Friends Provident – Sue Mills, Lead HR Consultant
Gothenburg, Sweden – Elderly Care – Britt-Marie Högberg (Leader in Elderly Care at Lundby, Gothenburg, Sweden); Rüddi Porsgaard, CEO and Team Coach at Strandska
HSBC – Steve Marshall
KPMG – Claire Mear and Louise Buckle
Legal Services Commission – Elizabeth Crosse
National Health Services Institute for Innovation and Improvement – Sue Mortlock, Head of Coaching
North West Employers and NHS NW – Lynn Scott
Metropolitan Police – Hyacinth Daly
National College for the Leadership of Schools and Children's Services – Mary Ann Stuart and Glyn Rawlins (Third Field)

North West Employers Organization – Liz McQue, Coach Organizer, North West Employers
OXFAM – Liz Lambert, Head of Organizational Development
PricewaterhouseCoopers – Barbara Picheta and Lyn Chambers
RWE IT – Jamie Mowatt
Royal Navy – Commander Mike Young
Singapore Civil Service College – Paul Lim
Southern Railways – Zoey Hudson, Leadership and Behavioural Development Manager and Matt Watson, HR Director
Tesco – Maxine Dolan, Head of Leadership Development
Thames Valley Police – Steve Chase, HR Director
Thompson Reuters – Stephen Dando, HR Director, Anne Bowerman, Head of Leadership Development, and Claire Goodman, Head of Coaching
West Midlands Local Government Association – Gil Schwenk, Bath Consultancy Group External Trainer
Yell Group – Karen Lloyd, Coaching and Development Manager
Yeovil District Hospital Foundation Trust – Alison Rayner, HR Director, and Gavin Boyle, Chief Executive

Introduction: Coaching at a crossroads – the challenge for chief executives, HR directors, heads of coaching, internal and external coaches, managers, coach trainers, and researchers

As I sit here writing this book, I want to reach out and engage you, the reader. I try to picture who might be sitting around this table with me. Are you a chief executive who is wondering how coaching could help you make a difference to your organization? Perhaps you are a coach who enjoys the individual coaching relationships in your work, but becomes frustrated that you cannot have more of an impact on the organizations that employ you. Or a human resources (HR) or learning and development manager who knows coaching is an important part of developing your people, but wants to ensure that coaching is aligned with the other many strategies you need to engage with but are unsure how best to do this. Maybe you are an internal coaching champion who wants to know how to convince your senior managers that coaching can add significant value to taking forward the business or organization.

You are all welcome to the table and to this book where I am committed to engaging with your difficult and challenging questions. I have spent the last four years talking with people, like yourselves, who know coaching has so much more to offer, but have serious questions about how together we can make this happen.

I want to invite you to participate with me in an inquiry that engages with the question:

> What can coaching uniquely do that the world of tomorrow needs?

We all know that the world faces ever more complex challenges and that those who lead our public and civil society organizations and commercial companies are facing larger, more complex, and interconnected challenges than ever before. To grasp these challenges, we need to grow our individual and collective capacities, both intellectually and emotionally, to lead organizations and people in aligned responses.

This very evident need has led to a great growth in leadership development, which has become a multi-billion dollar worldwide industry. However,

I would contend that leadership development approaches are not evolving and developing as fast as the challenges we face, and there is an increasing gap between what is needed and what is provided.

Coaching at a crossroads

Coaching has been one of the most significant developments in leadership and management practice in the last thirty years. Yet today, people are beginning to question whether coaching delivers the required individual and organizational value.

The growth in coaching provision has been worldwide, but especially in Western Europe, North America, and Australasia. Now over 70 per cent of large companies in these areas are using coaching as a major form of management and leadership development (Zenger and Stinnett, 2006; and see Chapter 1). To date, coaching has focused mainly on the individual development of leaders and managers. Even with recession many organizations continue their commitment to coaching as an effective way of ensuring individual and organizational learning and adaptability. We are also seeing the spread of coaching internationally, with strong growth in Eastern Europe, the Middle East, and Asia Pacific.

The next phase of development in coaching will be fundamentally different, with a growing demand for coaching not only to serve individual development, but also the strategic and commercial development of the whole organization. What is required is a subtle yet profound paradigm shift in the work of coaching at all levels whether delivered by internal or external coaches. Until now, coaches have focused on the person or team they are working with and seen them as their client. In the new paradigm of coaching, I believe we need to see this person or team not as a client we face, but as a partner with whom we stand side by side. Coaching then becomes a joint endeavour in service of a third party, whether that be increased leadership capacity, organizational change, a strategy being implemented or a team better able to serve its many stakeholders.

This book is the last of my trilogy addressing how coaching can move into the next phase of its own development. In 2006, I wrote with my colleague Nick Smith, *Coaching, Mentoring and Organizational Consultancy: Supervision and Development* (Hawkins and Smith, 2006), which addressed the needs for linking coaching, mentoring, and organizational change and the key role for supervision in continuing to raise the quality of all three practices. Then I wrote *Leadership Team Coaching* (Hawkins, 2011a), in which I argued that the world needs more collective leadership, high-performing leadership teams, and effective team coaches that can work with the whole team, not only on their internal functioning, but how they engage with all their stakeholders. Here, in part three of the trilogy, I focus on finding ways for coaching to have a greater impact on taking forward the organizations in which it happens and coaching moving beyond what happens in the coaching room to becoming a style of managing, leading, and engaging with all stakeholders.

I have written this book for all of you who want to be part of this next phase in the development of coaching. Whether you are a chief executive, HR director, head of organizational development or leadership development, coaching manager, internal or external coach, coach trainer or writer, you all have your part to play in ensuring that coaching is linked to the overall development of the business and to creating real value.

I will now look at the specific challenges that face different groups. While each group has its specific concerns and agenda, there is a need to be involved with each other. Ultimately, we are all engaged because we want to see organizations, and those who work in and for them, flourish and thrive. Work involves us for a good deal of our lives, so it pays to ensure they are places where we can give of our best and continue to learn and develop as well as furthering the organization's aims. Workplaces are also a key aspect of the sustainable communities we need for a flourishing society and essential to addressing the economic, social, environmental, and political challenges that now face our world.

The chief executive's challenge

Many chief executives and HR directors I have spoken to over the last few years have been tremendously proud of the growth of coaching in their organizations. They are, however, concerned about the organizational benefit, sustaining the offering and evaluating the return on investment.

To address these concerns I first ask them: 'How many coaching conversations do you think happen every month in your organization?' Very few have a clear idea but most will estimate that it is in the thousands, particularly if you include coaching conversations by line managers and not just external and internal coaching. Then follows a simple but challenging question: 'How does your organization learn from these thousands of coaching conversations?' They are usually puzzled but curious as to how coaching can lead to organizational learning and demonstrable organizational benefit. If coaching is to realize its potential as an important tool in developing the leadership that is needed in twenty-first century, then this must be addressed. Leadership is not an isolated activity but exists within a context.

In my teaching I stress that one of the key distinguishing features of coaching that separates it from counselling or psychotherapy at work, is that coaching always has at least three clients: the individual, the organization, and the relationship between the two. Coaches, coach trainers and supervisors, those of us writing and researching in this field, the coaching professional bodies, *and* the employing organizations are responsible for addressing this balance. This means giving much more attention to how to ensure organizational benefit. In the employing organizations, the responsibility for ensuring maximum benefit from the investment in coaching starts with chief executives. They, together with their board and fellow directors need to ask searching questions, including:

1. To be successful, what sort of organizational culture do we need and how is it linked to a coaching culture?
2. To create such a culture, what sort of leadership culture do we need?
3. What is the gap between the leadership we need to take this organization forward and the current leadership capacity?
4. How can we best utilize and target coaching to fast track our future talent and develop our key current leaders?
5. How can we utilize coaching as part of how we maximize our engagement, the on-going learning and development of our people, and our performance management, improve our morale, and radically improve our impact as an organization?
6. How and where should we invest in coaching and how will we evaluate our return on investment?
7. What is the mix we need of individual, relationship, team, and whole-system coaching?
8. How do we integrate our coaching strategy with our business strategy, our organizational development plans, our leadership strategy, and our talent strategy to ensure maximum synergy and effectiveness?

Rarely do chief executives and other directors ask these important strategic questions up front, but wait for their HR director and staff to make proposals, often on the back of personal enthusiasm, and then later wonder why the impact of coaching is underwhelming. This book is written to help you not only ask the right questions at the beginning of the process, but also to learn how you can best sponsor and encourage the development of a coaching culture, and regularly review, evaluate, and add value to the process as it develops.

The human resources director and leadership and development manager's challenge

Even if the board is not asking the right strategic questions, that is no excuse for the HR director. You should be looking for good practice and the best way to impact the business strategy through a range of effective and aligned people strategies.

In the past, HR managers have suffered from line managers who outsourced to them the hard conversations about performance and behaviour that they found too difficult or embarrassing to handle, or lacked the emotional intelligence to handle well. In turn, HR managers outsourced to external executive coaches what they found too difficult and too embarrassing to handle themselves. In supervision I often question executive coaches about why they were having the challenging conversation, which should have been had with the line manager and immediate colleagues.

One new senior HR manager of a large retail organization wanted to know what was happening in the area of coaching. She discovered that nobody could tell her:

- who was having coaching;
- how long they had been having it;
- how much was spent on coaching;
- what the criteria were for someone being offered coaching; and
- what criteria were applied in selecting external coaches.

As she delved a little further, she discovered that over £1 million was spent on coaching with no way of targeting this spend or evaluating the return on the investment.

This book is written to help HR directors and managers look at how they can best develop and align coaching activities, and also integrate the creation of a coaching culture with their other key HR strategies and initiatives such as: recruitment; people; learning and development; talent development and promotion processes; leadership development; performance management and team development. In fact, there are very few HR processes where coaching and creating a coaching culture do not have a part to play.

Heads of coaching and coaching champions

Increasingly, large organizations are appointing a head of coaching and smaller organizations or those with more limited resources are appointing a coaching champion. Cleary, this person has a key responsibility for looking at how all coaching activities, whether delivered by external coaches, internal coaches or line managers with coaching skills, are developed and integrated and how they best impact on people development and organizational effectiveness. They need to know the best practice in all aspects of coaching strategy, coaching development, coaching practice, and ways of creating a coaching culture. I hope this book provides you with much that can accelerate this learning, as well as help you choose, plan, integrate, review, and evaluate your own organization's coaching processes.

Internal coaches

Many organizations are recruiting, training, and developing a community of internal coaches. In some organizations these may be drawn primarily from the HR community, but other organizations have recognized the benefits of having coaches drawn from all parts of the business, who give two or three hours a week of their time to coach staff from other parts of the organization.

This book will address some of the key questions internal coaches should ask, including:

- How can we best pool our collective knowledge of the organization and talk to the senior executives about what we see happening, while maintaining appropriate confidentiality with our fellow internal coaches?
- How do we manage to combine our day job with being an effective internal coach and continue to learn and to develop in both roles?
- How do I get my line manager to recognize and reward the value I deliver in the coaching work I do?

External coaches

External coaches have been very busy practising their craft with little time to stand back and address the wider systemic issues of their profession. Large organizations are now employing fewer external coaches as they develop their internal coaching capability. In this age of austerity in many countries this trend is increasing, with many public service organizations imposing a complete ban on hiring external coaches, while recognizing that the need for coaching is increasing. At the same time, people who have been made redundant or taken early retirement are training as coaches. This means that competition for coaching contracts will increase dramatically.

As mentioned above, I also meet many external coaches who enjoy their individual coaching in companies, but get frustrated when they become aware of the many limiting patterns in the organizations they work for. They often have difficulty in finding a way of helping the wider organization or system to address these patterns and use their coaching skills better to support organizational learning and improvement.

For external coaches to add value, not just to their individual executive clients but to the wider organization, they need to play their part in helping the organization link the coaching activities to the wider business agenda and create a sustainable coaching culture. In this book, I will address the following questions that I am asked by many external coaches:

- How can we better impact the wider organization?
- What needs to change in our coaching to create greater value for the individual coachee and their organization?
- How can we best support and partner the internal coaches and the coaching organization?
- How do I offer to the organization my perceptions and reflections on the organization having worked with a number of their senior people?

Manager as coach

As well as developing internal coaches, many organizations are recognizing that coaching is a key aspect of every leader and manager's role. Every leader and manager has to deliver value through the people they lead and manage. They need to help those people constantly: improve their performance, effectiveness, and efficiency; adapt their work to the changing context, both externally and within the organization; and align their efforts with the work of others.

A number of organizations provide short periods of training in coaching skills for all managers, and some progressive organizations ensure that managers receive supervision on how they coach their staff and the teams they lead. Often coach managers ask:

- How can I effectively coach all my staff in the limited time I have in my busy schedule?
- How can I do this 'virtually' as I often have to travel?
- How do I continuously improve my coaching, when I have had limited training and limited opportunity to do further training?
- How do I coach my team collectively so that they can coach each other and we can create a self-supporting team coaching culture?

In this book, especially Chapter 9, I will show how the best organizations are addressing these concerns of the manager who is developing a coaching style to the way they manage, often under considerable time and work pressure.

Coach trainers, researchers, and writers

There are hundreds of books on coaching and a plethora of training courses ranging from one-day programmes to diploma, masters, and doctoral programmes. The majority of the books and training programmes work from 'inside-out': they start with the personal awareness of the coach, then develop coaching skills and techniques, and then relationship skills, and only then go on to explore the organizational and systemic context in which coaching takes place. Educationally this makes perfect sense. However, there is an urgent need to rebalance the whole profession with a focus that approaches the work from 'outside-in' and from 'future-back' (Hawkins, 2011b). In this approach, one starts from the challenges currently facing the world and explores what this requires of organizations; then what organizations will require from their leaders and managers; and then what development is therefore required. Only then can we usefully ask:

- How can coaching best enable the development of current and future leaders and managers as well as the effective development of organizations to meet the challenges of tomorrow?
- How does coaching need to change to do this?
- How does the way we organize and deliver coaching need to change?

Coaching has grown up in the world of psychology and personal development and has to date been very individually focused. The challenge now is to add to this individual focus a wider engagement taking into account the global and social context, the organizational development agenda, the organizational culture and the team, and the team development agenda.

In this book I address all those who are involved in training, researching and writing about coaching, and offer what I see as the new and wider agenda for the next stage of the development of the coaching profession – an agenda that is looking at how coaching can deliver greater organizational learning and value, create greater alignment between the individual, team and organizational development agendas, and which has better forms of evaluation. Issues concerning training of coaches are addressed through the seven steps of the coaching culture (Chapters 4–10), areas of continuous personal and professional development and supervision in Chapter 12, and ways of creating more effective evaluation and research in Chapter 13.

Those working in organizational development

To date, coaching has mainly been associated with individual learning and development. However, here I will show how coaching and coaching processes have a key role in all aspects of organizational development, including:

- how best to utilize team coaching for leadership teams, boards, project teams, sales account teams, management teams, etc.;
- how coaching can help the strategy process;

- the impact of a coaching approach on customer relationships and stakeholder engagement processes;
- the use of coaching to specifically increase organizational agility, change readiness, leadership engagement, and effective change processes.

In this book, I demonstrate what organizations are doing and can do to develop a more effective coaching strategy that delivers usable and measurable organizational benefit.

How to approach the book

The book starts by setting the historical and current context of coaching. It charts its exponential growth over the last thirty years and describes how it now faces a number of key challenges. In particular, the challenge of linking the many different coaching activities now occurring in organizations to the wider development of the organization and ensuring that coaching delivers real and lasting value.

To meet this challenge, I outline in Chapter 2 the overall framework that needs to be in place including a robust coaching strategy, which is further explored in Chapter 3. Chapters 4–10 then address each of the seven steps to creating a coaching culture in turn. Chapter 11 explores how these seven steps can be integrated and aligned to the 'relational value chain' and some of the major traps and pitfalls that might be encountered on the way and how these can be handled. Finally, Chapters 12 and 13 address the need to ensure that the organization does not just develop lots of coaching activities, but develops the quality, depth, and effectiveness of the coaching through continuous personal and professional development, supervision of all coaching and regular assessment, review and evaluation processes.

The book concludes by bringing together the various threads and revisits the challenges facing the coaching profession outlined here. I explore some of the possible scenarios for the next stage of development of coaching and how these might be addressed. At the core and heart of the coaching endeavour are quality conversations and generative dialogue that create better places to work, higher performing organizations, and a greater ability to respond to the many challenges in our global environment. The book ends by considering this core of our work and how we can all contribute to taking it forward.

Conclusion

In a time of economic austerity, recession, and restricted credit lines, it is inevitable that every line of cost will be regularly reviewed. There will be increasing pressure for coaching to demonstrate its return on investment and increase its capacity not only to develop leaders in a cost-effective manner, but to be part of effectively developing the organization to better succeed in a volatile and fast-changing world. For coaching to step up to this challenge it requires engagement from a wide range of stakeholders: chief executives; HR directors and managers; all those involved in learning and development, whether for individuals, teams, organizations or whole systems; external and internal coaches and line managers; and the wider coaching profession. No matter which of these groups you belong to, I welcome you to the table and to this important joint inquiry.

1 Setting the context: the growth of coaching and the challenges it now faces

Introduction

Although coaching in organizations has been around for over thirty years, it is the last twenty years that have seen an exponential growth in coaching in the UK, North America, parts of Europe, and Australasia. In the last few years we have seen a marked growth in coaching throughout most other parts of the world. The 2007 International Coach Federation coaching survey estimated that the coaching industry generated US$1.5 billion dollars in revenue worldwide, and Carr (2005) estimated the number of coaches worldwide to be approaching 30,000. Coaching has become a significant and regular part of most leadership development activities (Corporate Leadership Council, 2003), and Zenger and Stinnett (2006) estimated that 70 per cent of organizations with formal leadership development initiatives were using coaching as a key ingredient. The 2009 annual survey of the UK Chartered Institute of Personnel and Development showed that over two-thirds of the 539 companies who responded were using coaching.

This growth has been accompanied by a parallel upsurge in the number of coaching training bodies. Carr (2008) estimated that in North America there were fewer than twelve established schools of coaching in 1999, rising to 291 by July 2008 and 'eleven competing associations claiming to be the "standard-setter" for coaching' (Carr, 2008: 114). There has also been an exponential growth in the literature, with a 300 per cent growth in published articles in scholarly journals from 1994–1999 to 2000–2004 (English, 2006; see also Grant and Cavanagh, 2004). There was also a massive upsurge in the number of books and other publications on different aspects of coaching.

Why has coaching grown?

The UK Chartered Institute of Personnel and Development carried out extensive research into the buying side of coaching (CIPD, 2004, 2008, 2009) and identified ten main reasons why companies are continuing to turn to coaching (CIPD, 2008):

- demand by employees for different types of training;
- as support for other learning and development activities;
- as a popular development mechanism;
- a rapidly evolving business environment;
- the features of modern organizations;
- life-long learning;
- the need for targeted, individualized 'just-in-time' development;
- the financial costs related to poor performance of senior managers/ executives;
- improving the decision making of senior employees; and
- individual responsibility for development.

Another driver has been the need to develop leaders and managers who are far more skilled in relationships and engagement than has ever been necessary in the past. Hooper and Potter (2000) wrote that the key issue facing future leaders is

> unlocking the enormous human potential by winning people's emotional support . . . our leaders of the future will have to be more competent, more articulate, more creative, more inspirational and more credible if they are going to win the hearts and minds of their followers.

In the instant information age, product and service quality can easily be learnt and copied by others. Many organizations realize that it is becoming less possible to differentiate themselves from their competition purely on product quality. They need to differentiate how they relate to their customers, clients or service users. Having a great brand, product or service is essential but no longer sufficient for success in either the commercial world or the public and civil society. How one delivers the service or product and engages the customers and service users is as important, if not more important.

A recent study has shown that even in manufacturing there has been a marked shift away from a purely product-centred strategy to one based on engagement and relationship throughout the product lifecycle (CapGemini, 2010). This requires a focus on what I have termed the organization's 'lived brand' – how the organization is perceived by its customers and stakeholders through daily interaction. We also know that how employees treat their customers is most influenced by how they themselves are related to by their managers and leaders. Clark (2002) shows how the organizational climate as perceived by employees can affect how they engage with customers, which in turn can affect customer retention. In Chapter 11, I will explore how coaching can be set in the context of understanding the organization's 'relational value chain', that is how the quality of the relationships inside the organization affects the quality of relationships with customers, service users, and other stakeholders, which in turn impacts on the perceptions of the organization and its ability to create shared value.

There is also a social change in western societies towards less deference to authority and higher expectations of how individuals are related to at work. So, leaders across all sectors find their employees increasingly expect them to be more motivational and inspirational. This becomes even more critical in those sectors where there is a 'war for talent'. This combination of factors requires leaders and senior managers to have much greater relationship skills and emotional intelligence (EQ) than was previously necessary. Coaching provides leaders with a development process for focusing on growing the emotional and relational aspects of their leadership capacity, by addressing specific relationship challenges and how the leader might handle them differently.

The change in organizational learning

Coaching has also been a key part in the revolution in thinking about how managers and leaders learn. Influenced by the work of such writers as Senge (1990), Pedler et al. (1991), Argyris and Schön (1978), Hawkins (1991, 1994, 1999), and Garratt (1987, 1996, 2003) on the learning organization, there has been a move away from seeing learning and development as something that only happens on off-site taught courses, to a greater focus on incorporating learning and development into the day-to-day challenges of the workplace. I have built on the work of Honey and Mumford (1982) to develop a simple grid that shows four domains of learning (Figure 1.1).

Development no longer sits predominantly in the lower right quadrant of Figure 1.1. There is now a recognition that learning on the job needs to be linked to learning off the job. In various research studies on global best practice in leadership development that I have been engaged with (see Hawkins and Smith, 2006: 101), we have found that leadership development is most effective when it is:

- based on a clear vision of the leadership culture and capabilities needed for future success;
- focused on developing leadership teams and not just individual leaders;
- combined with developing individuals and teams within a context of integrated strategy and culture change;

14 CREATING A COACHING CULTURE

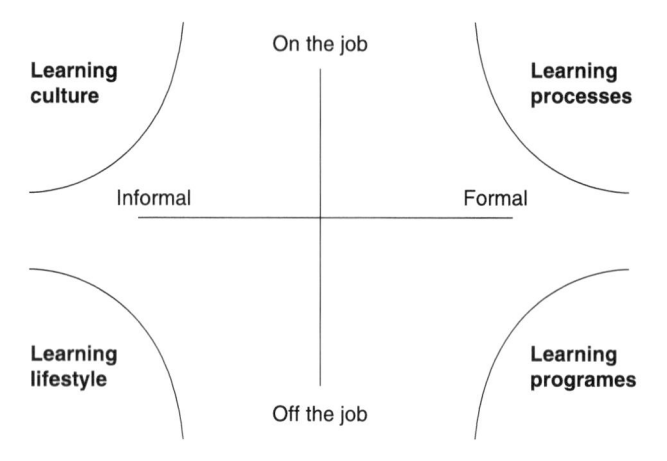

```
                      On the job
  Learning            |              Learning
  culture             |              processes
                      |
         Informal     |     Formal
  ──────────────────────────────────────
                      |
                      |
  Learning            |              Learning
  lifestyle           |              programmes
                      Off the job
```

Figure 1.1 Four domains of learning

- attended to in the whole action learning cycle of combining action, reflection, new thinking, informing new planning and rehearsal, leading to new action;
- provided with real-time strategic challenges to leadership learning groups or teams, which require them to relate in new ways and think outside the box;
- required that leaders work across any sector boundaries that get in the way of delivering excellent value for customers;
- in partnerships in ways that also reflect on the partnership working;
- creates just-in-time learning so that people have the need for the learning activity or input, just before they obtain/receive it.

A number of the organizations interviewed for this book talked of trying to operate the 70:20:10 principle whereby 70 per cent of development should be supported learning on the job, 10 per cent formal development programmes, and 20 per cent coaching and mentoring that links the other two activities. Looked at from the perspective of Figure 1.1, the four dimensions of learning as applied to coaching now appear as in Figure 1.2.

Most organizations are continuing to maintain or increase their investment in coaching activities. However, there has been a marked shift in where the coaching investment is being made. A number of organizations are having more of the formal coaching 'on-the-job' done by trained internal coaches (upper right quadrant). Also many organizations are adopting a coaching style approach for 'business as usual', in other words how managing, leading, team meetings, and engaging stakeholders are carried out (upper left quadrant). There is also a growth in coaching linked to other forms of training

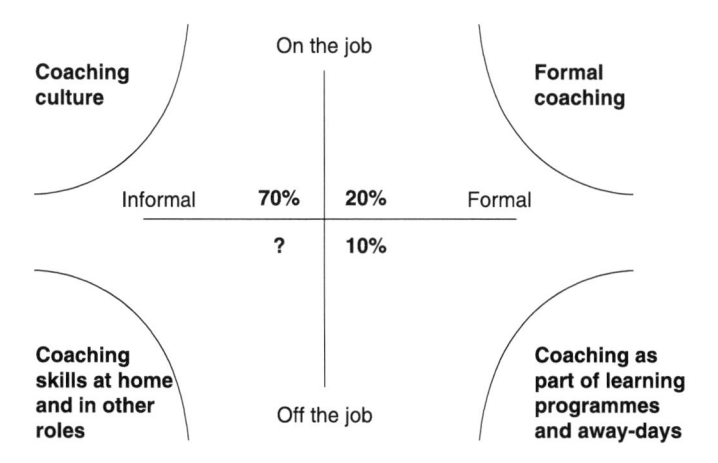

```
              On the job
Coaching    /     |     \    Formal
culture    /      |      \   coaching
          /       |       \
         /        |        \
    Informal   70% | 20%   Formal
    ─────────────────────────────
                ?  | 10%
         \        |        /
          \       |       /
Coaching   \      |      /  Coaching as
skills at home\   |     /   part of learning
and in other  \ Off the job/ programmes
roles          \  |    /    and away-days
```

Figure 1.2 The 70:20:10 principle

and development (the lower right quadrant of formal, off-the-job learning), particularly leadership development programmes, and involving leaders and managers coaching in the wider community (lower left quadrant).

The current challenges

While the use of coaching has grown apace, the field and the nascent profession are fraught with many challenges.

Thirty years ago, coaching was predominantly a remedial activity for executives who were either not performing or needed to address difficult aspects of their personality. Senior managers would 'outsource' their difficult conversations, asking the HR department to address the manager they did not want to confront. The HR department would then often find this too difficult a challenge and 'outsource' the difficult conversation to an external coach. This may be somewhat of a caricature, but the pattern is one that many coaches and HR departments recognize and one that still exists in a few organizations.

Twenty years ago, coaching became more focused on developing executives with potential, and 'having a coach' was a mark of progress and no longer associated with having a problem.

Ten years ago, the activity of coaching gradually started to be re-sourced in-house, with coaching being carried out by trained internal coaches, with more of the development conversations occurring between the employee and their line manager. At the same time, coaching has moved from focusing on individual development to also include the team, the wider organization, and the organization's stakeholders.

16 CREATING A COACHING CULTURE

In the midst of these wider changes the coaching profession has been struggling to define what coaching is and decide:

- who is most appropriate to do it;
- what training coaches should have and how they should be assessed and accredited;
- and, most importantly, what coaching is there to achieve and how its contribution should be evaluated.

A recent *Harvard Business Review* Research Report delivered the following challenge: 'The coaching field is filled with contradictions. Coaches themselves disagree over why they're hired, what they do, and how to measure success' (Coutu and Kauffman, 2009: 26). I have written elsewhere (Hawkins, 2008, 2009) about the challenges facing the coaching profession, all of which I address in this book and then return to in the final chapter. These include:

- coaching as an 'undefined basket of very different activities' (see Chapter 2);
- where and when it is best to use coaching (see Chapters 2, 4, and 5);
- matching coachees to the right coaches (see Chapters 4 and 5);
- coaching being over-focused on personal development and not delivering organizational benefit (see Chapters 7, 8, 9, 10, and 13);
- the need for more effective team coaching (see Chapter 7);
- continuing to develop the depth and quality of coaching through continuous personal and professional development, supervision, and evaluation (see Chapter 12);
- the need for much better evaluation and research (see Chapter 13);
- integrating and aligning the wider coaching profession (see Chapters 7 and 14).

Conclusions

This chapter has provided some historical and contextual perspective on the exponential and global rise in coaching over the last thirty years. This growth has brought in its wake new challenges for the field and for the nascent profession of coaching. In addition, the current global economic climate following the global economic crisis of 2008–2010 has ushered in an age of austerity, where private sector, public sector, and civil society organizations need to tighten their belts, and rigorously investigate every line of expenditure and the return it is providing. At the same time, the crisis was not just economic, but a crisis in virtue and values, with public outrage at the self-serving behaviour of company executives and non-executives, politicians, and all those in positions of leadership. The need for effective leadership development has increased at the very time that the resources to spend on it have decreased. Is coaching ready to respond? Coaching has a great opportunity to rise to the challenges inherent in the current world situation, but will only do so if it can use these challenges to raise it own game, become more strategic, and discover ways of delivering measurable value to teams and organizations, as well as personal development to individual leaders and managers.

The challenges are either a threat or an opportunity for coaching. In the final chapter, I offer three possible scenarios of what may happen in the field of coaching in the future, in the context of these challenges. I hope this book helps all involved with coaching from all positions to seize the opportunity of a step change in the value coaching can provide.

PART 1
The foundational pillars

2 What is a coaching culture? The key ingredients

Introduction

For executive coaching to progress successfully to the next stage of its development, it needs to move beyond the confidential one-to-one personal development process to be a key ingredient in, and contributor to, the organization's development and the creation of higher organizational performance and stakeholder benefit. One senior executive I spoke to said: 'It is time for coaching to come out of the closet and be part of the bigger change journey.'

In this chapter, I present an overarching framework for how coaching can approach this transformational threshold in its own development, and how coaching and organizational benefit can be linked much more strongly. This will then provide the scaffolding for the different elements that will be explored throughout this book. I end by providing a map for how each part of this coaching architecture is picked up in the different chapters of the book.

What is a coaching culture?

In my interviews I asked a number of people what they were trying to achieve in creating a coaching culture and their vision of what success would look like. I also have looked at the literature on coaching cultures, including Clutterbuck and Megginson (2005), Hardingham et al. (2004), Caplan (2003), and many others. From all these elements I have arrived at a new aspirational definition of a coaching culture:

> A coaching culture exists in an organization when a coaching approach is a key aspect of how the leaders, managers, and staff engage and develop all their people and engage their stakeholders, in ways that create increased individual, team, and organizational performance and shared value for all stakeholders.

To give more colour to this definition, I then reflected on my research with different companies to draw out what the different levels of an organizational coaching culture could be, using the five levels of culture, outlined in Chapter 3.

Artefacts: The organization espouses the importance of coaching in its key strategy and mission statements and coaching appears as a key competency and capability for all leaders and managers.

Behaviours: A coaching style of engaging is used in one-to-one as well as team meetings, as a way of encouraging both problem solving and continuous team and personal development. There is a focus on the collective endeavour of the team and the organization and its stakeholders.

Mindsets: There is a prevalent belief that you get the most out of people, not through telling them what to do, or through advocacy and explanation, but through engaging them with the issues and challenges and helping them think through the choices and options. There is a belief that nobody has all the answers, but through inquiring together we can arrive at better responses to new challenges than by thinking alone.

Emotional ground: The mood of the organization is one of energy, with high levels of personal engagement and responsibility, where every challenge is an opportunity for new learning, and problems are addressed through engaged relationships. There is high challenge and high support for all employees with a real focus on helping individuals and teams to realize their individual and collective potential.

Motivational roots: At the well-spring of such a culture are people who are both committed to their own lifelong learning and development, and who believe in other people and their potential to learn continuously. There is also a belief that collective performance can improve through learning and development. These motivational roots are also fuelled by a belief in the power of dialogue and collective exploration. There is a belief that together we can create ways forward better than any of us can do by ourselves.

This book will explore the steps necessary to move towards this being a reality in many different types of organization.

Developmental stages in creating a coaching culture

Surveys indicate that relatively few organizations believe they are deriving the full benefits of executive coaching (Jarvis et al., 2006; McDermott et al.,

2007; BlessingWhite, 2008; Peterson, 2010b). The reasons that are given include:

- lack of clarity of the purpose of coaching in the organization;
- lack of focus on where and when coaching would be most beneficial;
- inconsistent quality of coaches;
- absence of good contracting between coach, coachee, and line manager; and
- lack of good evaluation of outcomes.

Writing primarily from an American perspective, Peterson (2010b) suggests that organizations typically go through four stages in their use of external coaches:

1. *ad hoc* coaching – driven by individuals;
2. managed coaching driven by a champion or sponsor;
3. proactive coaching driven by business need;
4. strategic coaching driven by organizational talent strategy.

The first stage is often driven by the enthusiasm of a few senior executives who have found coaching personally beneficial and recommend it to others, and who locate coaches by personal recommendation or through people they know. Suddenly, the organization can discover that they are spending a large amount of money on coaching, which is being paid for from local budgets, with no financial or quality monitoring. When Maxine Dolan was put in charge of coaching at Tesco, she was shocked to discover that the organization was spending over £1 million a year on coaching with no way of monitoring the appropriateness or the effectiveness of this spend.

In the second stage, organizations often appoint a key individual, either a senior executive or a senior member of the HR or learning and development department, to lead the production of a more central plan for coaching and expenditure in this area. This usually moves on to a recommendation for coaching to be better linked to the business agenda and more proactive in who should have coaching and when (stage 3 of the model above). In time, organizations may then target their coaching spend even more by linking their coaching to (a) the leadership, leadership development, and talent strategies, and (b) the organization's culture change and other current change processes. This takes the organization into Peterson's stage 4, where there is a strategic coaching approach.

Knights and Poppleton, in their research for CIPD (CIPD, 2008), argue that these stages need not be sequential, and that later stages are not necessarily better, as it depends on the type of organization and its developmental needs. They observed three ways of structuring coaching services, which they termed:

- *centralized and structured*: providing a structured, standard, and consistent service across the organization;
- *organic and emergent*: where the aim is to be responsive to specific needs and preferences in the organization as they arise;
- *tailored middle ground*: where the organization chooses a mix of the above two approaches, so as to have some consistency in service, while responding to specific organizational contexts and needs.

The authors concluded their research by stating:

> One size clearly does not fit all in relation to organizing coaching services. What's important is having a clear understanding of the organizational context for coaching, then establishing the enabling processes that are congruent with that understanding and intent.
> (Knights and Poppleton, 2008: 10)

I agree with Knights and Poppleton that 'one size does not fit all', and their argument for the approach to organizing coaching being tailored to the needs and style of the particular organization. However, I think they are in danger of creating fixed polarities between the centralized and organic and also between the structured and emergent. I would contend that sooner or later, it is necessary for every organization that invests in coaching to transcend both of these 'either-ors'. This does not mean creating a 'tailored middle ground', but an approach that transcends the false dichotomy by creating three foundational pillars, which:

- provide a clear unifying coaching strategy, linked to the mission and current business strategy, while encouraging flexibility of coaching provision in different parts of the business and a constantly evolving, developing, and learning coaching approach;
- link coaching to the wider organizational culture change, while realizing that developing an organizational culture is never a linear journey from A to B. Rather, it is a journey that, at its best, discovers more about the culture and what needs changing as it attempts to bring about that change;
- have an integrating infrastructure that while giving clear direction and decisions on resources from the top and the centre, those at the top and centre are constantly learning and being informed by what is

happening in all the evolving coaching activities throughout the organization and the wider system.

Developing the three pillars

Creating a robust and sustainable coaching strategy and culture requires it to be built on strong foundations. I would suggest that if any of these three key pillars is missing, there is a danger that coaching can become marginalized, or swept away in the next round of organizational cuts, restructuring or new initiatives.

1. Coaching strategy

The first pillar is creating a coaching strategy that is not just another policy document among hundreds of others in the organization, but one that is firmly grounded in the organizational mission, the current business strategy, the organizational development plan, and linked to all the people development policies (leadership, management, talent, etc.). This strategy needs to be developed collaboratively, constantly updated as the context and the practice change and develop, and communicated to everyone in the organization. Processes for doing this are explored in Chapter 3.

2. Aligning the coaching culture with the wider organizational culture change

The second pillar ensures that creating a coaching culture is aligned to the wider changes in the organizational culture. For any organization to thrive it

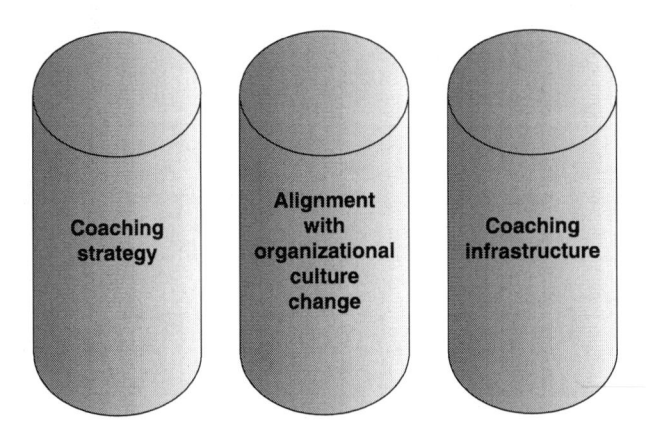

Figure 2.1   The three pillars.

needs to be developing its strategy at the same speed or faster than the world in which it operates is changing. However, the even bigger challenge for the organization is to develop its culture at the same speed as it is developing its strategy. Organizational cultures are pervasive and inherently conservative and can be a drag on all forms of strategic change unless they are carefully developed. Creating a coaching culture is not an end in itself, but a means to an end. A coaching culture is a key part of creating a more general culture of continual learning and development that will enhance the capabilities and capacities of all staff, managers, leaders, teams, and the organization as a whole. Learning and development and increased capability and capacity are also not ends in themselves, but in service of individual, team, and organization performance. High performance, in turn, is in service of creating greater shared value for the organization and all its key stakeholders. Ways of aligning the contribution of coaching to the important task of developing the organizational culture are also explored in Chapter 3.

3. Coaching infrastructure

The third pillar that anchors all the activity of coaching at work is establishing and maintaining the necessary governance, management, and involvement of all parties that will provide a sustainable, robust, and integrated operation. There are several key aspects of such an infrastructure:

A strong sponsorship/steering group. This group ideally needs to include: a representative of the senior leadership team; the HR director; senior executives from the different business units and functions of the organization; the coach manager; and some young potential leaders of the future who represent an important customer group of the coaching. It is important that this group has both clout and visibility in order to demonstrate that coaching is not a temporary project, or merely an HR initiative, but located at the centre of the organization and driven by senior line managers. The sponsorship/steering group needs to act as the board for all coaching activities providing the high level decisions, scrutiny and alignment to the key strategies and development of the business. Like all good boards, they should be involved in creating the coaching strategy, allocate the resources and drive quality evaluation and review processes.

A management group. The management group need to drive, co-ordinate and integrate all the coaching processes and activities. The composition of this group will depend on the size of the organization and the stage of development in coaching. At a minimum there needs to be a full-time coach manager or part-time coaching champion. However, over-reliance on one central driving force is dangerous and full of risk. This person will soon become over-burdened and the coaching enterprise will become too dependent on their efforts, capability and retention. If they leave, the development of a coaching culture can go backwards or flounder. A small effective group is far preferable.

A community of practice. Good governance and management are critical but not sufficient, and the third key part of this pillar is a community of practice of all those who are providing the coaching. This community, as I will show throughout this book, needs to be more than a group of trained and quality suppliers. They need to be true partners in creating a coaching culture committed to the development and success of the wider organization. They need to be motivated, engaged, integrated and aligned to the business agenda. Their commitment must not just be to the individuals they coach, and the development of their own practice, but to the development of the coaching culture and community within their organization and how it learns and develops. To create such a community requires investment of time and resources. Throughout Chapters 4–10 I will show how such a community can be established and sustained, with examples from organizations that have successfully done so.

The three pillars are rarely put in place before an organization begins to establish coaching activity. Indeed, many of the organizations studied only addressed the need for these foundations once they realized they had a lot of coaching activity, without any effective integration or evaluation.

The seven steps

In *Coaching, Mentoring and Organizational Consultancy: Supervision and Development* (Hawkins and Smith, 2006), we suggested seven steps that are necessary for establishing a full coaching culture, while recognizing that very few organizations, if any, had successfully put them all into place. Since writing that book, I have interviewed, studied, and engaged with a wide variety of organizations, from several different countries and in different places on the journey to creating a coaching culture. In the light of what has emerged from these encounters, I have slightly amended the naming of some of the steps, while mostly finding validation for the approach and the importance for all seven steps.

In the six years since writing *Coaching, Mentoring and Organizational Consultancy*, there have been many developments, particularly in team coaching and ways of harvesting the organizational learning from the many rich and varied coaching conversations. Both these activities now feature strongly in Step 4.

The seven steps do not necessarily become established in the order they appear, although my research did confirm that this was the most frequently used sequence. In Chapter 11, I will explore different routes and order in establishing these steps.

One of the big challenges in sustaining the journey to becoming a coaching culture is that it is all too easy to focus on the many inputs and forget the outputs and outcomes. Like many long-term initiatives, the costs of investing in creating a coaching culture are mainly at the early stages, whereas the benefits are accrued further down the road. Having invested large amounts in the individual coaching of senior executives or developing a quality community of internal coaches, some organizations become impatient if they do not see the business benefits. I have helped a number of senior executives develop both patience and a bigger picture by showing them the seven-step model, and how the output benefits and business outcomes only start to emerge when the coaching efforts have been supported by some of the later steps in the coaching culture journey (Figure 2.2).

The depth of the foundation

Having established the seven steps, built on and supported by the three pillars, we do not have sufficient for a full coaching culture. If the organization stops here it will have created a strong infrastructure and lots of coaching activity and approaches, but be in danger of confusing producing quantity with ensuring quality.

Once coaching is underway it is important that the skills are constantly developed, the coaching relationships deepened, with the support of on-going development opportunities, coaching supervision, and quality evaluation processes. These ways of deepening the practice of coaching and the quality of what it produces are addressed in Chapters 12 and 13. They provide the bedrock on which the pillars and the seven steps sit (Figure 2.3).

Putting the framework together

This framework provides a map for both coaching strategy in organizations and the steps to creating a coaching culture. It provides also a map through the book. Figure 2.4 shows how each part of this framework is covered by different chapters

It is important, however, to remember the map is not the territory and the process is never simple and linear. Organizations I talked with constantly described putting a coaching culture in place as being more like spinning plates than progressing step by step. None of the elements remains still and constant

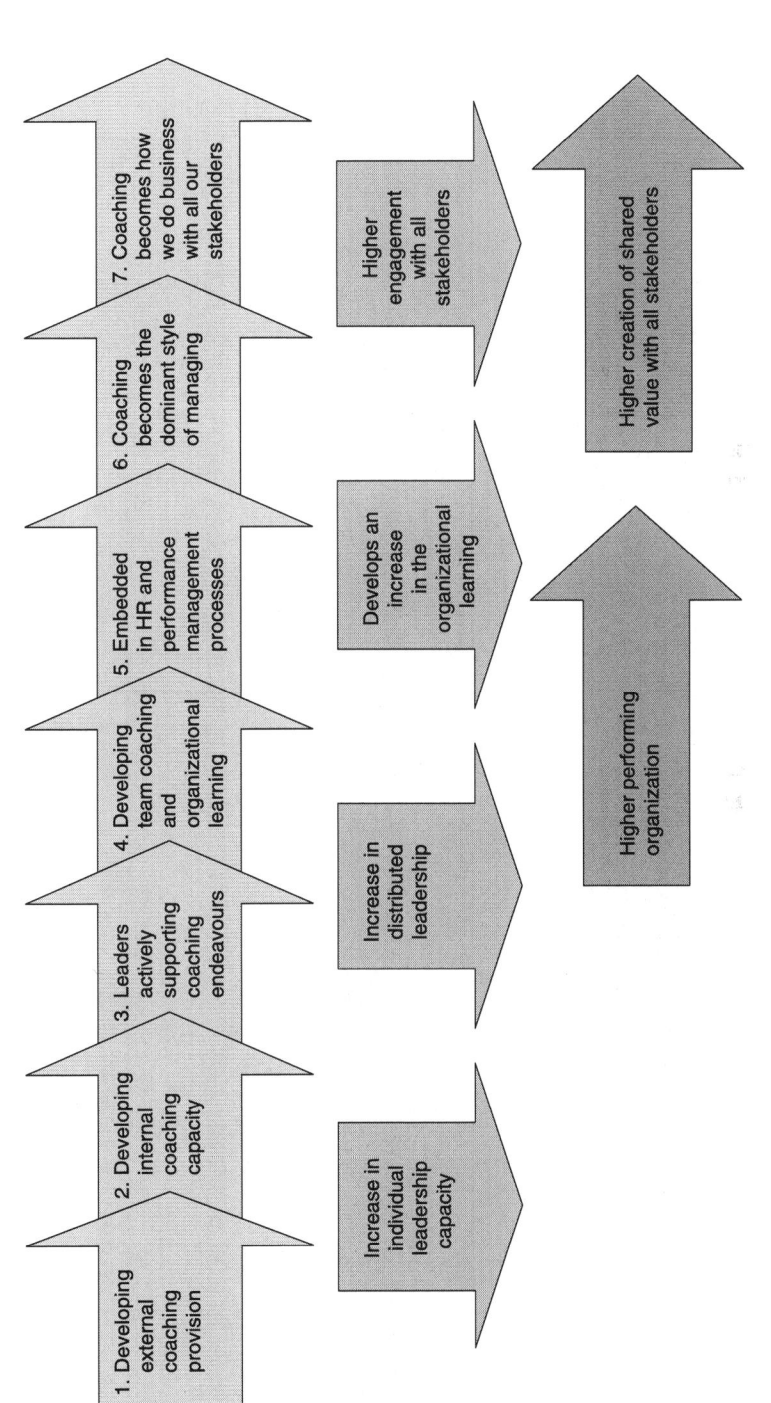

Figure 2.2 Developing a coaching culture – outcomes.

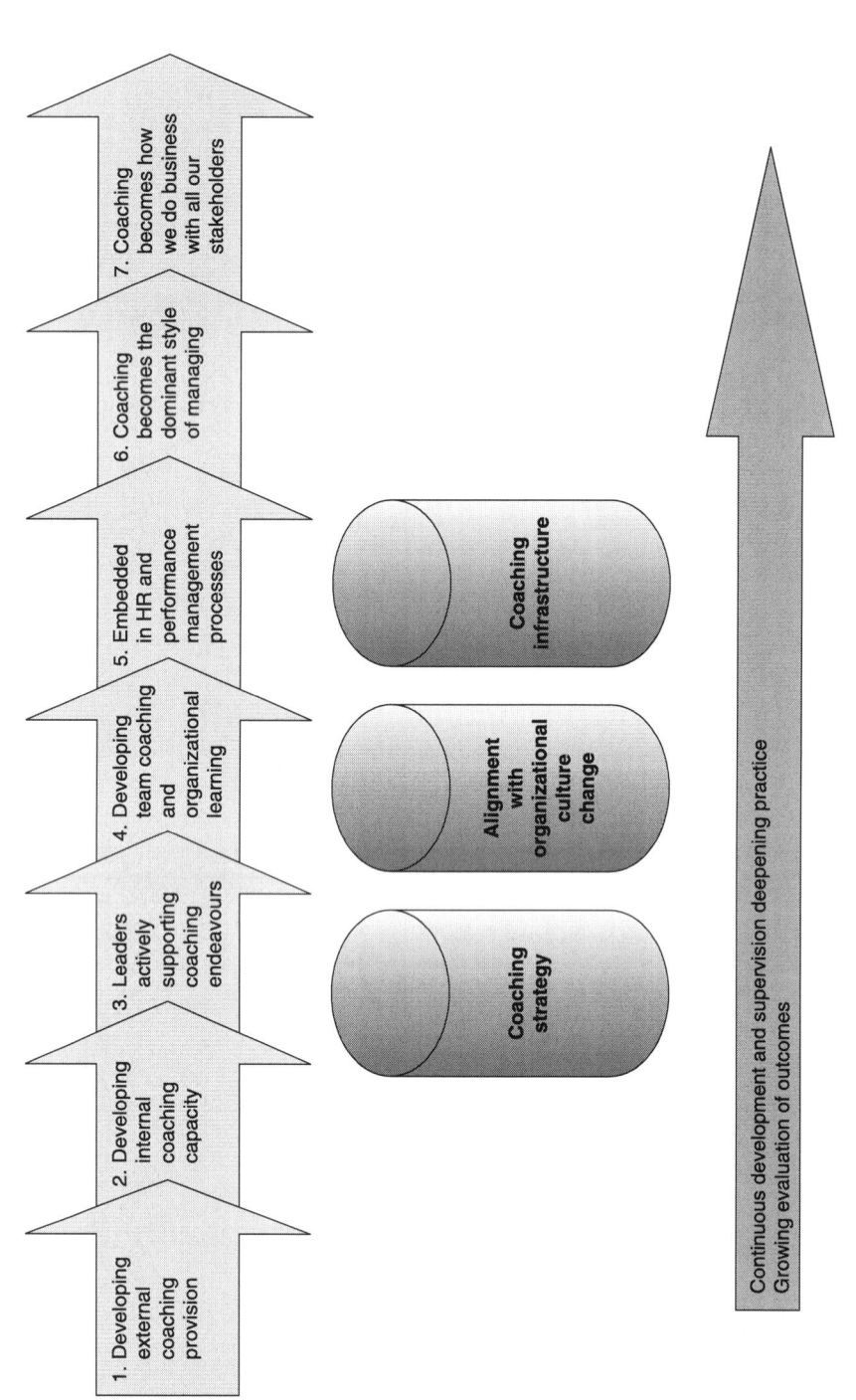

Figure 2.3 Coaching strategy: steps to creating a coaching culture.

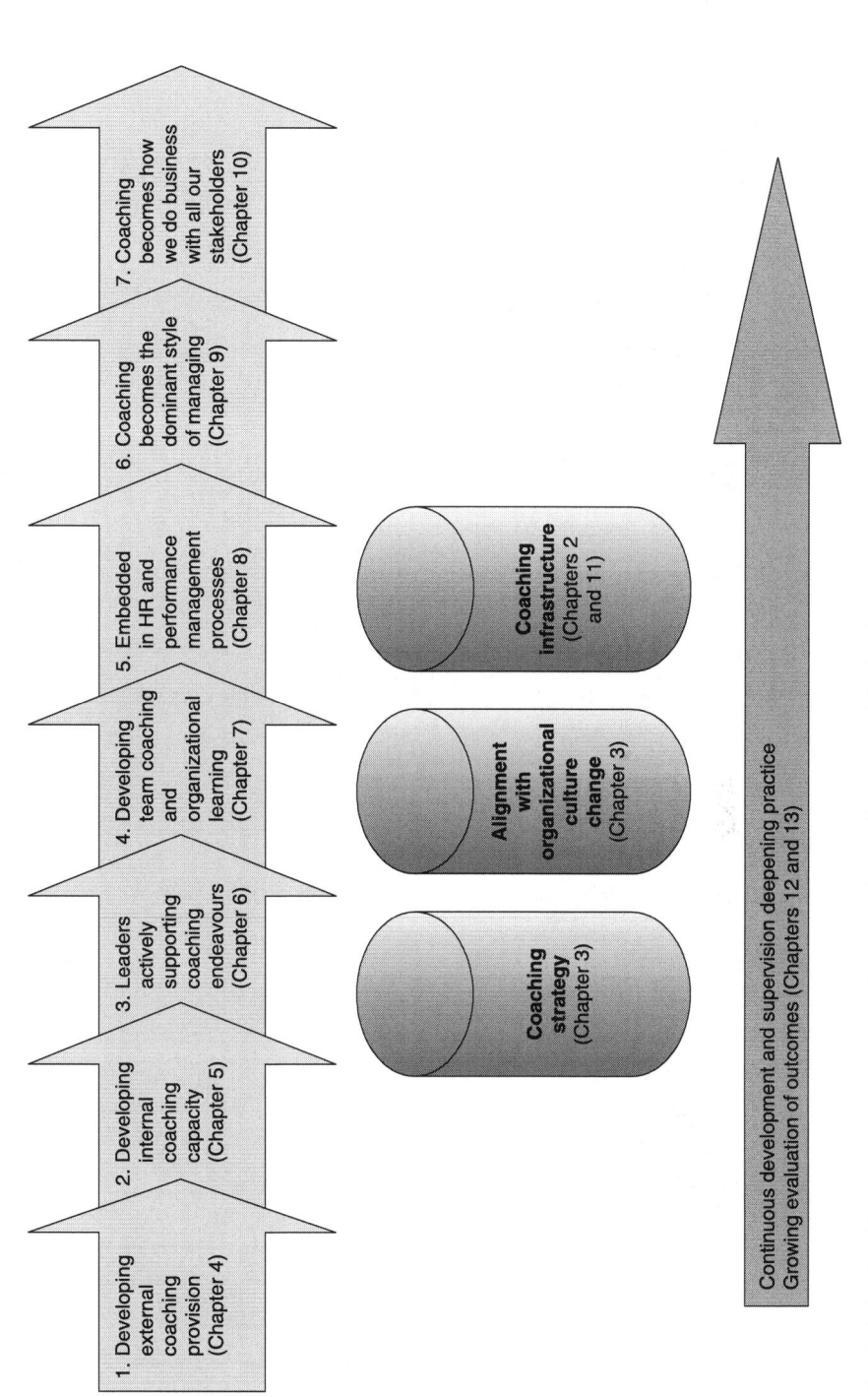

Figure 2.4 Coaching strategy: steps to creating a coaching culture map of the book.

as the next step is put in place, but need to be attended to and adapted in response to the fast changing world around them. However, a number of organizations reported how useful it was to have the map, as it had helped them stand back and see where they were on their journey, notice what they were not seeing, provide new avenues they had not yet explored, as well as recognize all that they had achieved. Several organizations also found the framework very helpful in educating their senior leaders, in seeing how all the different activities and initiatives fit together and how the whole is greater than the sum of the parts.

3 Creating a coaching strategy and aligning it to the wider organizational culture change

Introduction

In this chapter, I outline the steps to creating a coaching strategy in line with the business strategy and the culture change that an organization is undertaking. I show that there are two foundational steps (A and B below) that need to be undertaken by the wider organization to establish the pillars of business strategy and culture change mentioned in the previous chapter, and then eight steps that need to be undertaken by those responsible for developing the coaching strategy itself. Examples from leading organizations illustrate these steps.

A. Ensuring there is a clear business strategy on which to build the coaching strategy

It is foolish to create a coaching strategy without first ensuring there is the requisite strategic foundation upon which to build it. Too often I have discovered well-intentioned coaching strategies developed by HR departments or developed for them by their consultants that exist in a vacuum and have no integration with the organization's mission, business strategy, organization development strategy or leadership and talent strategy. These coaching strategies are often riding on the wave of their own enthusiasm for coaching and the support of one or two key sponsors. A coaching strategy can never be an end in itself, only a means to an end. Without the clear business linkages, these initiatives will struggle to be sustained and even if they do keep going, will fail to deliver the full business benefit. A good coaching strategy stands on the foundational pillar of the organization's mission, business strategy, and organizational development plans (see Figure 3.1). These should provide the bedrock for exploring the strategy needed for coaching in the

34 CREATING A COACHING CULTURE

Figure 3.1 Foundations of the coaching strategy.

organization, as illustrated by Ernst & Young in their Coaching White Paper in November 2007.

> ### Case study: Ernst & Young: The business case for coaching
> As a professional services firm, we realize that our talented people are our most important asset. If we can improve the way we attract, develop and motivate our people, we will drive efficiency, quality and client service.
>
> Ernst & Young's global positioning articulates that we will achieve the potential of our clients and the communities we serve by achieving the potential of our people. We will only achieve the potential of our people by stimulating a culture that allows for individual development and growth in a rapidly changing environment.
>
> By embedding a true coaching culture . . . into the way we manage our people and our business research shows we can expect to:
>
> - Increase the effectiveness with which we support our people to develop their skills and realize their potential.
> - Help our people adapt to new challenges, role transitions and change.
> - Reduce turn-over.
> - Attract new talent to our organization
> - Improve our business performance.

B. Establishing the required culture change

For an organization to be successful, every time it embarks on significant changes to its strategy, it must attend to how to change its culture to deliver the new strategy, for as Peter Drucker so dramatically expressed it, 'Culture will eat your strategy for breakfast' (this is also used by Mark Fields, President of Ford Motor Company). Failure to address the culture of an organization is one of the main reasons that organizational transformation efforts fail so often. It has also been identified as one of the main reasons the majority of mergers and acquisitions fail to achieve their financial targets and why knowledge management strategies fail.

One of the main reasons that organizations fail to address culture change is because culture is hard to define and measure. Organizational culture is a concept that is widely used, and most people think they understand it, yet it is subtle and elusive. This is because culture is not a thing that you can take out and measure, but a connecting pattern that pervades all aspects of an organization. It is very hard to recognize one's own culture, for as the Chinese say, 'The last one to know about the sea is the fish'. One's own culture becomes taken for granted and part of one's way of seeing the world, thus it is difficult to step outside it to evaluate it properly. Many definitions of culture have limited the concept to the behaviours of people in the organization. The most commonly used definition is: 'How things are done around here' (Ouchi and Wilkins, 1985). Although culture may manifest itself through patterns of behaviours in an organization, the culture is more deeply rooted in the shared meaning making, motivations, assumptions, and emotions of an organization.

To capture this simply, I created the following definition:

> Culture is what you stop noticing and take for granted when you have worked somewhere for over three months.
> (Hawkins, 1997)

I have also built on the work of Ed Schein (1985) and others to develop a five-level lens through which to view organizational cultures (see Hawkins, 1997; Hawkins and Smith, 2006) (see Figure 3.2).

The other limiting perspective is that organizational culture is often limited to looking at what happens inside an organization and fails to recognize that the organization's culture is enacted and constantly changed in the thousands of interactions with its many stakeholders. In light of this, I now offer a new definition of organizational culture:

> Culture resides in the habituated ways of connecting that an organization repeats. Culture resides not just inside the organization, but more

36 CREATING A COACHING CULTURE

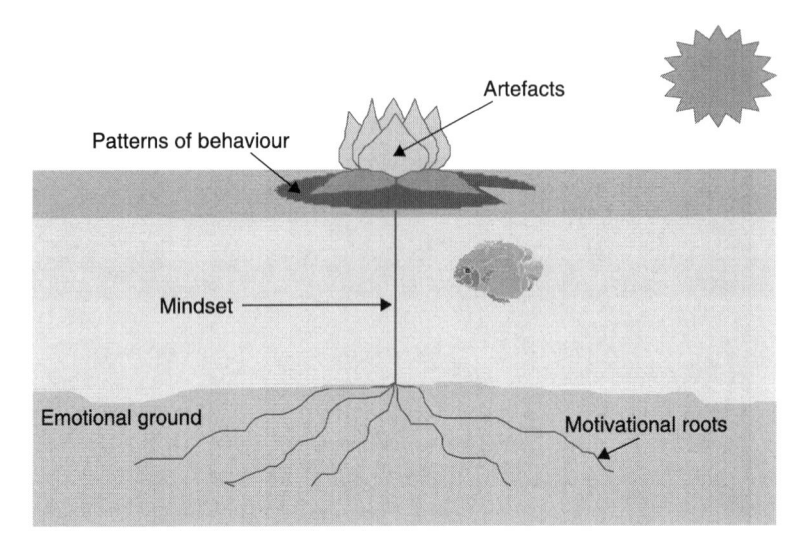

Figure 3.2 The five levels of culture.

importantly in the relationship patterns with all the key stakeholders (the lived brand).

Most of the successful organizations I have worked with and studied have recognized the need to constantly develop their culture in line with their changing strategic direction, which in turn needs to constantly change to respond to the changing needs of all the various organizational stakeholders. Organizational culture change is therefore a key aspect of organizational agility and transformation. Creating a coaching culture cannot stand alone as a change initiative but must be in service of the wider culture change of the organization. In Chapter 11, I explore this further when I introduce the concept of the 'relational value chain', which can provide an overarching approach for linking coaching to the wider culture change and organizational responsiveness to the changing world in which organizations operate.

The coaching strategy workshop

In helping organizations develop their coaching strategy, I often arrange a workshop with those responsible for coaching, as well as key HR directors and managers and some senior line executives as well as future leaders.

For this workshop to be successful, it is important that we start from the bigger organizational picture and explore from the 'outside-in'. I usually start by having all the elements of the mission, strategy, and organizational development plans pinned up around the walls. This needs to include the important foundations on which the coaching strategy can be built (Figure 3.1). Also, on one of the walls, I may have the map of the wider culture change journey of the organization.

All of these elements set the context for exploring how coaching can make the most effective contribution to the organization's development and success.

1. Establishing the external perspectives and needs

To bring these data alive, I will ask those attending the workshop to split into pairs or groups of three and represent the different stakeholders in the wider system in which the organization operates. I ask them to step into the shoes of one particular stakeholder group and say what they both appreciate and find difficult about the organization, and what they wish could be different. The group can then summarize what the key messages are from across the stakeholder group – both what they appreciate and what needs to be different.

2. Establishing the internal perspectives and need

It is then possible to look at the different groupings within the organization: senior leaders, managers, support functions, front-line staff, and so on. Again, it is useful to split the workshop members into small groups. Each group steps into the shoes of one of the group of employees and voices what development is needed to help them to contribute more to taking the organization forward towards meeting these stakeholder needs as well as the organization's espoused strategic goals.

From this work we are able to start with 'the end in mind' – knowing the difference that coaching is in service of creating. I ask the workshop members to summarize this before we move on to look at what is currently happening.

3. Mapping what is already happening – it may be more than you think!

A coaching strategy should not just be about the future, but should address how what the organization is aiming for is already manifest in some parts of the organization. To do this, the organization needs to carry out an 'appreciative inquiry' on best practice of what is already happening in all aspects of coaching within the organization.

> Appreciative Inquiry seeks out the very best of 'what is' to help ignite the imagination of 'what might be'. The aim is to generate new knowledge which expands 'the realm of the possible' and helps the partners of an organization envision a collectively desired future and then to

carry forth that vision in ways which successfully translate intention into reality.

(Cooperrider and Srivastva, 1987)

This may involve looking for examples of good performance management, people development processes, effective team development, and informal training and development conversations where the leaders and managers are unaware that what they are doing constitutes coaching.

4. Deciding the best contribution from individual and team coaching

Sometimes I create a large fishbone diagram to map the creation of the coaching strategy. At the head I ask the participants to place the key organizational aspirations and objectives. At the tail I ask them to write up all the current coaching activities. This clearly leaves the body of the fish, showing what needs to be developed over the next period of time for coaching to make a greater and more aligned contribution to the organization's development and success.

1. The organization's strategic and development aspirations
2. The current state of coaching
3. Suggested steps to get there placed on a time-line
4. Major coaching activities that need to be developed
5. Key ingredients for each activity

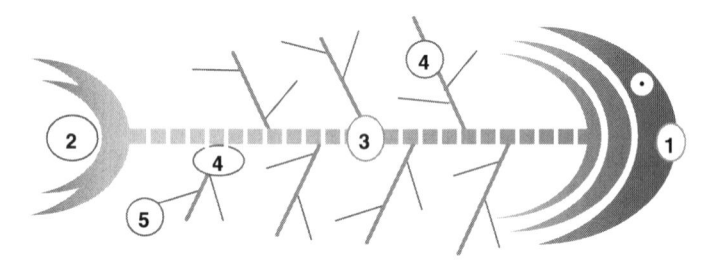

Figure 3.3 Fishbone strategy building.

Before the group can start to populate the key coaching activities that will best enable the journey from the tail of the fish to the head, it is important for the group to explore the areas where coaching can potentially make a valuable contribution. The group can use a brainstorm to generate these possibilities. The following is a list of the sorts of areas that might emerge:

- leadership development;
- support the 'on-boarding' of recruited leaders, in a way that accelerates their ability to create value for the company and increases retention rates;

- developing managers;
- preparation for career transitions;
- a coaching approach to performance appraisals and development reviews;
- the need to support and increase the speed at which the newly promoted leader is value-creating in their new role;
- developing high performing senior teams;
- shifting the leadership culture;
- board development;
- developing integrated and higher performing customer account teams;
- more effective project teams and better transformational change initiatives.

Once the list has been generated, the workshop participants can prioritize those they think will make the best contribution to the journey from the tail to the head of the fish – that is, from now to the required organizational outcomes.

The areas of highest priority can be placed along the spine of the fish, which can be used as a time-line. The first areas to be tackled will be near the tail and the later ones nearer the head. The time-line can have dates added to it, with the group deciding the speed at which they wish to progress through the activities. It is useful to use Post-it® notes, as these can be moved around as the plan develops.

Once the spine is populated, the workshop can split into small groups, each one taking one of the key priority activities and developing the side of the fishbone for that area. These should include: key aspects of the activity that need to be included, some early definite first steps, some quick wins that can be achieved, and who will lead, sponsor, and be accountable for this activity. Once the different teams have completed their creative work, they present their thinking back to the wider group and add their side of the bone to the main spine of the fish where it should appear on the time-line.

At this stage, the other workshop members may be able to build and add to the plans developed. In addition, the whole group will start to see connections between the different activities and explore how they can be integrated in the most effective manner.

There is a great deal of material and examples of good practice in Chapters 4–10 that can support the development of these different action areas.

5. Aligning coaching with other organizational, team, and individual development endeavours

There is a danger that coaching, and becoming a coaching culture, will be viewed as the flavour of the month, or this year's initiative, and like so many other initiatives before it, disappear and be replaced by next year's bright idea from the HR department! Another danger is that the coaching strategy becomes part of what is sometimes termed 'death by a thousand initiatives', whereby those working in the organization experience a constant bombardment of disconnected initiatives. To avoid this happening, it is important that the coaching strategy is constantly connected with the other change programmes occurring in the organization, and all of these change programmes are linked back to the organizational mission and strategy. The coaching strategy and policy should be able to illustrate how it is enabling the organization to achieve its goals and its change plans, and how coaching as a process is aligned with how the organization needs to be, in order to succeed. Thus it is important that once the coaching fishbone plan is completed, that the workshop participants pause and refocus on all the other current activities and initiatives in the organization. Then they can explore how to ensure that this plan is not only well aligned to the other initiatives, but where possible is integrated with them.

6. Consultation and piloting

By the end of the coaching strategy workshop, a draft strategy and plan can be formulated, but not yet printed and circulated. There needs to be a period of both consultation and fast-trial experiments to try out elements of the plan and learn further about how best to implement them. The consultation and feedback on the draft plan can usefully involve a series of different groupings: senior leaders, managers, possible customers of the coaching, potential suppliers, and other organizations further down the road of developing a coaching culture.

Several organizations I spoke to wisely decided to pilot some experimental coaching initiatives, and evaluate and learn from these, before going public with their coaching strategy. A member of one organization argued that if you raise the strategic flag before you are ready with activity on the ground, you are asking to be shot at! This echoes an early phrase that I use in talking about change management: that 'cynicism grows in the rift between rhetoric and reality'.

A member of another organization reported:

> If we just published our plans and aspirations, it would have been derided as another HR initiative and created cynicism or disinterest. The fact that we could show what had been achieved in some tough areas of the business made people sit up and take notice.

Members of several other organizations spoke about how important it is to ensure that they could show that coaching was linked to the best leaders and good managers improving their performance and coaching was thus not seen as a remedial process.

7. Creating the coaching strategy document

Once the organization has a plan that has been responded to by key groupings and some success has been achieved, it is ready to produce its coaching strategy, to make clear the why, what, how, who, where, and when of coaching in the organization.

The style and format will need to be matched to the appropriate style for the organization. Some organizations I interviewed used PowerPoint slides, others a short written policy. Whatever style is used it needs to be brief, simply expressed, and clear. At the same time it needs to show how it aligns coaching with the wider mission, business strategy, and overall development of the organization. From the wide variety of coaching policies and strategies that I reviewed, I would recommend a short document that covers the following.

1. An introduction that provides the organization's own definition of coaching and why it believes coaching will contribute to the success of the organization.
2. The organization's mission.
3. A summary of the current business strategy.
4. The key elements of the culture change journey and the organizational development plan.
5. How the above links to the people strategies, including leadership, management, and talent development plans.
6. The key part that coaching can play in supporting these various development initiatives.
7. The outcomes that coaching is planning to deliver for the organization, its development, and for the leaders, managers, and teams within the organization. These outcomes should be specific and measurable enough to be used to evaluate the effectiveness of the coaching investment (see Chapter 13 on evaluation).
8. What coaching will be provided for individuals, teams, and the wider system, and how it can be accessed by individual managers and leaders.
9. Who will provide the coaching – including external coaches, internal coaches, and line managers.
10. Where will this coaching be especially targeted and why.
11. How the coaching processes will operate.
12. How the coaching will be reviewed and evaluated.

Case study: The UK Foreign and Commonwealth Office
This large government department has always recruited some of the brightest and best-educated graduates in the country. There had been a well-developed

career structure and grades that employees gradually moved through. However, the world context was requiring much greater agility, relationship skills, transcultural competence, and collaborative working. The department wanted to have a more diverse workforce with greater emotional and relational skills and to move to a culture where all leaders and managers took responsibility for developing their staff.

Their 2010 Coaching Strategy started by linking the coaching to the FCO's people strategy, and the organizational purpose and strategy.

The purpose of this Strategy is to:

- provide a coherent **framework** for our coaching activities, linked to the People Strategy (Aim 1) and to other learning and development;
- pursue **'Value For Money' and focus** coaching investment on priority areas, using expensive executive coaching where it has most impact;
- suggest ways that coaching can **benefit the organization** more widely and deeply than just as a one-to-one development intervention;
- **communicate to staff** the purpose and availability of coaching and the way it is distinct from, for example, training, on-the-job tutoring and mentoring.

The definition of *coaching* we use in the FCO can be applied to specialist one-to-one coaching, interactions between line managers and staff and to group or team coaching:

> *'Coaching aims to help release potential and to improve performance, primarily through a non-directive approach in a structured discussion.'*

Our coaching activities are in direct support of People Strategy Aim 1:

> *'To build, equip and reward a dynamic, flexible and professional workforce to achieve the objectives of the FCO of today and tomorrow. To foster a culture in which our staff exemplify the behaviour we want: our traditional values of public service, honesty, professionalism, teamwork and integrity; together with greater ambition, creativity and confidence, and the right attitude to risk.'*

Here the organization is aligning the coaching strategy with both the culture change plan and leadership strategy. The FCO is also showing how they are going to produce better value for money, by switching more coaching investment from external coaches to internal coaching, but at the same time they also indicate that they will ensure they maintain quality by purchasing regular supervision for their internal coaches from external coaching supervisors.

8. Implement and constantly review and reassess

Once the coaching strategy is produced, the organization can continue to implement coaching activities in a way that is part of and contributes to the wider organizational strategy and culture change process. However, the coaching strategy will need to be continuously reviewed and evaluated in the light of both what is learnt from implementing the strategy and the constant changes in the wider organization and its environment. Also, one discovers far more about organizational culture as one tries to change it.

Conclusion

For the coaching strategy to be dynamic and more than a strategic plan that gathers dust on executive bookshelves, it need to be emergent, adaptive, and constantly developing through discovering what happens in action. We have now explored the twin pillars of creating a coaching strategy and aligning coaching to the wider culture change activities of the organization. These two separate but linked activities are not necessarily sequential. The two processes of developing a coaching strategy and a coaching culture are parallel and intertwined. The strategy, like a good map, informs the journey at each stage, but the strategy is a map of a territory, which, at best, is only half known. As the journey proceeds, the map has to be changed and redrawn. Also, as the journey proceeds, different people join the caravan, and the strategy needs to be recreated to include them and be in a language that they own and understand.

It is neither a quick nor easy process for an organization to develop a quality coaching strategy and a coaching culture. However, the returns for systemically developing a culture where coaching is part of everyday relationships can transform not only the performance, but also the value creation of the organization. The journey will take a good deal of investment in time and money, and for this investment to be sustained over several years, it will require some form of on-going measurement and evaluation process, not only of the outputs and increased capability, but also of the more tangible outcomes. Many leading small, medium-sized, and global companies are on the journey from employing coaches, to training internal coaches, to ensuring that 'coaching is how we manage', and is built into the organizational processes and systems. It is with the help of their stories that I will journey through the seven steps of creating a coaching culture.

PART 2
The seven steps

4 Step 1: Developing an effective panel of external coaches

Introduction

Not all organizations start their coaching journey by using external coaches, but it is the most common starting point. As one senior executive put it, 'We need to receive good quality coaching before we can do it ourselves'. Indeed, I would argue that learning to be an effective and proactive coachee is the first step to becoming an effective coach.

Many organizations first started using external coaches in an informal and *ad hoc* manner. Individuals asked their HR department who could provide them with some coaching, or found their own coach, through personal recommendation. This is not a bad place to start, but once it mushrooms in size, the organization can find it is employing a large number of external coaches in different ways, at different costs, and of variable quality. It is also unlikely that there will be a strong link between the individual coaching and the organizational development. In the Introduction, I quoted the head of coaching at a large retailer who discovered when she took over this role that the organization was spending over £1 million on coaching, with no idea of how they were managing this investment or what return they were getting from it. Her experience, when she shared it at a conference on creating a coaching culture, was echoed by a number of other participants.

Gradually, organizations have moved to employing fewer external coaches, and using them more consistently and ensuring that they are aligned to the organization's strategic direction and organizational development. There are many ways in which this has been implemented. Below I present a model I have developed that is based on some of the best practice I have encountered.

The stages in forming an external coaching resource

If an organization goes down the path of deciding to systematize its coaching, either in a centralized and structured way or using a tailored, middle-ground approach, the following nine stages can be useful in organizing external coaching provision to ensure the best organizational return (see Figure 4.1). I explore each of these sub-steps in detail.

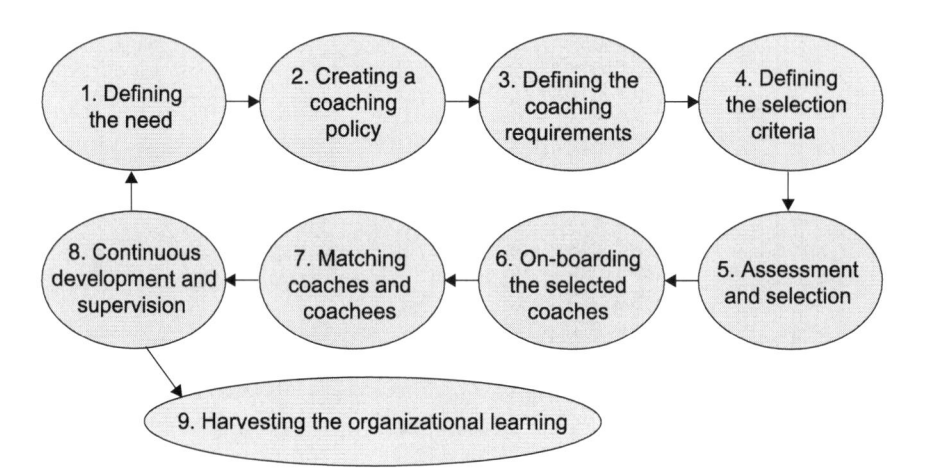

1. Defining the need
2. Creating a coaching policy
3. Defining the coaching requirements
4. Defining the selection criteria
5. Assessment and selection
6. On-boarding the selected coaches
7. Matching coaches and coachees
8. Continuous development and supervision
9. Harvesting the organizational learning

Figure 4.1 Creating and developing an effective pool of external coaches.

1. Diagnosing and defining the need

In developing a panel of external coaches, the first thing that the internal managers responsible for this task need to do is to start with the end in mind and develop with the organization an effective coaching strategy as outlined in Chapter 3. Having decided the outcomes by addressing these questions, the diagnosis can turn to the 'how', by addressing such questions as:

- What is the development journey needed to help the organization's leaders and managers to make this shift?
- How will coaching play a part in this wider development journey?
- What are the particular outcomes we would want coaching to deliver on this journey?

2. Creating a coaching policy and guidelines

The answers to the above questions can form the basis of an organizational coaching policy. A coaching policy is built on the foundation of the coaching strategy, and provides more detail of how coaching will be provided and contribute to the organization moving forward. These can be developed into a useful information sheet on coaching guidelines for all managers in the company. The coaching policy should include:

- *why*: the purpose of external coaching in the organization and how it is linked to the current business, leadership, and change strategies in the organization (see Chapter 3);
- *what*: the organization's definition of coaching;
- *who*: both who is eligible for external coaching as well as who the organization employs as external coaches;
- *when*: coaching is most useful (e.g. at transitions in role, linked to attending leadership programmes, preparing for future role, etc.);
- *how*: the processes of applying or being selected for coaching, being matched with a coach and contracting, reviewing, and evaluating the coaching;
- *what is expected*: the business, performance, and personal outcomes that the organization expects and that the individual can expect from coaching;
- *where*: to go for further information or for pursuing coaching options (e.g. performance or development review with the line manager, HR, coaching manager, etc.).

A good example of a coaching policy and guidelines is that developed by Thomson Reuters Executive Coaching Services, as they make it very usable by both HR staff working with different parts of the global business as well as executives looking on-line for a coach:

> The purpose of these guidelines is to define when executive coaching is appropriate and how to use this development intervention to best effect.
> The guidelines cover the following points:
>
> 1. What is executive coaching?
> 2. When to consider using executive coaching
> 3. How to ensure that a coaching engagement is effective
> 4. How to set up executive coaching
> 5. The cost of executive coaching
> 6. How to establish which executive coach to use
> 7. The role of HR

3. Defining coaching requirements

Having mapped the 'why, what, who, when, where, and how', we can turn to the question of which coaches are appropriate for the organization:

- What sort of coaches and coaching can best deliver the required organizational outcomes?
- What coach profile will best suit the organization?
- What level of experience, training, and accreditation is required?
- What combination of fit with our organization is required, while maintaining enough distance to bring in challenge and difference to help our leaders on the change journey?

4. Setting coach criteria

There are many sources an organization can consult for generic criteria for quality coaches. Many of the professional coaching bodies, such as the Association for Professional Executive Coaching and Supervision, the Association for Coaching, the European Mentoring and Coaching Council, and the International Federation of Coaching, list their own criteria. A number of coaching textbooks contain detailed sections on coaching competences, capabilities, and capacities (see Hawkins and Smith, 2006, Chapters 12 and 13; Passmore, 2010). These can be adapted by each organization to fit its own coaching requirements.

Executive coaching requires three fundamental and integrated capabilities of a coach, which I describe as a three-legged stool (Figure 4.2). The first leg comprises skills in the craft of coaching and establishing and maintaining effective coaching relationships. Every coach should have completed professional coaching training and be actively participating in continuous personal and professional development. The second leg is psychological understanding, especially in the areas of adult learning and development, personality types, learning preferences, and psychological conditions which may necessitate referring the coaching client for more specialized help. The third leg provides an understanding of organizational behaviour and the world of business. This requirement may be met by the coach having previously worked as an executive, or by the coach having completed an MBA or other business or organizational behaviour qualification.

For the stool to be effective, the three legs need to be connected, and good coaching supervision should provide the connecting seat of the stool, but only if it is provided by a coach supervisor who themselves is experienced in all three legs (see Hawkins, 2006, 2010, 2011b; Hawkins and Smith, 2006; Hawkins and Schwenk, 2011). This function of joining the legs together also involves coaches having a good systemic understanding, one in which they can identify and attend

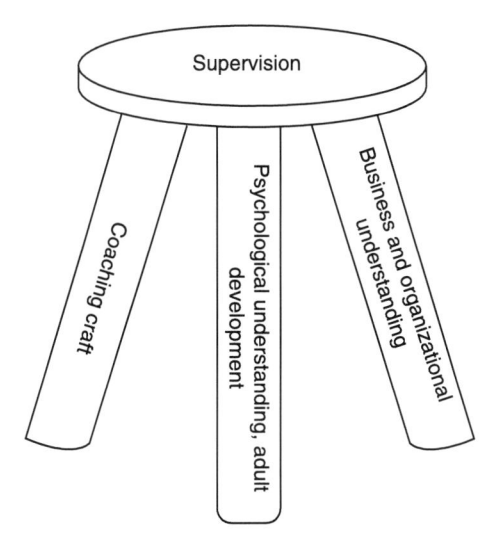

Figure 4.2 The coaching stool.

[Stool diagram with seat labeled "Supervision" and four legs labeled: "Coaching craft", "Psychological understanding, adult development", "Business and organizational understanding"]

to the interconnections between the individual, team, departmental, organizational, and wider stakeholder and system dynamics (see Hawkins, 2011c).

5. Selection

It is important that the organization is not only clear about what sort of coaches it requires (profile), but how many and what their terms of employment are likely to be. Without this there is a danger of the organization wasting a lot of its own time and resources and that of prospective coaches. With these steps undertaken, the organization should be able to advertise in a way that only relatively suitable and interested coaches will apply. However, if the criteria are too demanding or not sufficiently inspiring, some of the better coaches might not apply. It can be fruitful to approach coaches directly who are already known to be highly effective and suitable and invite them to submit an application.

Many organizations are surprised by how many coaches apply to be on their register. For example, HSBC had over 350 applicants for their coaching panel in 2008. The NHS Institute, which had more than 150 applicants for their first panel in 2006, received 1152 expressions of interest and 328 full applications for their second panel in 2009 – a daunting selection process! The first task is to score the applicants against the desired coach profile. Figure 4.3 provides an example of a coach profile form, drawn from several I have looked at. A framework such as this can be used for short-listing the applicants.

Area	1. Desired requirement	2. Applicant's score	3. Weighting of element	4. Weighted score (2 × 3)
Previous coaching experience				
Coach training and recent CPPD				
Relevant business/sector experience				
Business qualifications				
Membership of professional bodies				
Professional indemnity insurance				
Psychological training or experience				
Professional supervision				
Model of coaching				
Ability to handle ethical dilemmas				
Qualities and personal attributes necessary to match to the internal values				

Figure 4.3 Example of a coach profile form.

A number of different selection processes can be used for those short-listed, depending on the time and resources the organization can afford to devote:

- a short presentation by the coach on their approach to coaching, the models and processes they use, and how they believe they could add value to the organization;
- one or more in-depth interviews with the HR and coaching managers and also with senior executives who are potential recipients of the coaching;
- a live observed coaching session with a volunteer from the organization;
- a written reflection by the coach on both the interview and their coaching session;
- written or verbal answers to how the coach would approach a number of prepared possible coaching situations;
- an interview with the coach's supervisor to obtain a verbal reference (this was used by the NHS Institute as part of their assessment in 2009).

It should also be remembered that good coaches will have gone through a number of these selection processes, so if they are made too long and demanding, it may both reduce the number of good coaches wishing to proceed and also eventually add to the professional cost for coaches and hence the cost of coaching.

It is important that the interviewers are helped to use questions that do not just test the ability of the coach to do 'coach interviews', but help draw out the strengths, weaknesses, and particular approach of each coach interviewed (McGurk, 2008). In reviewing the selection process used by one international bank, I enquired what questions helped them separate the coaches they accepted (33 per cent of those interviewed) from those they turned down (67 per cent). They offered two open questions:

- Please describe an ethical dilemma you have faced in your coaching, and how you dealt with it.
- Please tell us about a time that you have used supervision to improve the coaching you were doing with a client.

They informed me that it was the same coaches who were able to provide meaningful answers to both questions.

The other factor that distinguished the successful coaches in the bank's assessment process was the congruence between their description of their coaching approach and what they actually did in the coaching demonstration – whether there was an alignment between their espoused theory and their theory in use (Argyris and Schön, 1978).

In our CIPD research on coaching supervision (Hawkins and Schwenk, 2006), we found that in addition to asking a coach whether they were receiving supervision, it was necessary to ask:

- Who do you receive supervision from?
- How often do you have supervision?
- Can you describe a time when supervision has transformed how you were working with a client?

A number of organizations have also chosen to outsource the selection of their external coaches and/or the management of their external coach panel. This is sometimes combined with the same provider, ensuring that all coaches continue to meet the requisite criteria and are given supervision geared to the needs of the particular client organization. This is true in particular of large global organizations, which find it difficult to recruit, quality assess, and keep aligned a global panel of coaches.

> In 2010, Carol Braddick carried out research on 'trends in executive coach selection' with input from forty major buying organizations and nearly 300 experienced executive coaches. Her research showed that most buyers and coaches were seeing a greater rigour emerging in coach selection and that buyers had a greater awareness of coaching and how it could best add value.
>
> Braddick discovered that the most significant elements that organizations looked for in executive coaches were prioritized in the following order (in parentheses we show the percentage of organizations who believed this to be essential, followed by the percentage who rated it as 'of benefit'):
>
> - recommendation and or referral from trusted source (53%, 45%)
> - business experience (other than running own coaching business) (53%, 38%)
> - coaching model and approach (48%, 40%)
> - supervision by a qualified supervisor (40%, 35%)
> - track record of continuous professional development (35%, 45%)
> - coaching qualification (33%, 55%)
> - accreditation by a school or professional body (33%, 53%)
> - membership of a professional body (26%, 51%)
> - personal knowledge of coach (25%, 55%)
> - contributions to the coaching field (5%, 53%).
>
> This supports earlier research by Underhill et al. (2007), who showed that organizations value the business experience of external coaches more than their coaching qualifications.
>
> When it came to selection processes, Braddick found that the most favoured by both organizations and coaches was a background review, followed by an interview, and that assessment centres were far less used and produced much greater polarization of views about the benefits they produced. Only three of the 40 organizations had used assessment centres with a further six considering doing so. Over half the coaches reported getting valuable insight from taking part in assessment centres, while others were clear they would not apply to be coaches in organizations that used assessment processes.

6. Bringing the selected coaches on board

Best practice organizations ensure there is some form of induction, briefing or 'on-boarding' event for the coaching panel appointed. This should be undertaken by a senior executive who sets the coaching requirements in the context of the organizational mission (purpose, strategy, core values, and vision) and explains how the coaches can best add value to both the organizational and individual clients they will be working with. The event should also cover:

- the process by which the coaching will be conducted – coach matching, initial meetings, three-way contracting, review, evaluation, reports, etc.;
- what feedback and psychometric instruments are used in the organization (360 degree feedback, Myer-Briggs, Firo-B, Belbin, etc.) and how this will be made available and can be used in the coaching;
- what evaluation criteria and feedback processes are used to assess both the coaching and the coach;
- how the collective organizational learning from the coaching will be harvested and how the coaches will be involved with this;
- general contractual arrangements, including confidentiality, handling conflicts of interest, ethical boundaries, etc.;
- invoicing and methods of payment;
- how the coaches will be kept updated on the changes in the organization and in the coaching policy and operations.

It is important that this is not just an information-giving induction process, but one that attends to building a committed community of coaches, coach managers, and senior executives who have the joint endeavour of taking forward the organization, its strategy, culture, and leadership.

7. Matching coaches and coachees, and aligning coaching to the organizational needs

Different organizations adopt different approaches to matching individual clients to appropriate coaches:

Open book self-selection. The organization publishes a directory of the coaching pool, with a short biography of each coach, providing relevant background, experience, approach, location, and contact details. Prospective coachees contact their choice directly to arrange an exploratory meeting and inform the central organizers.

Open book joint selection. As above but the prospective coachee contacts the central coaching manager and discusses their preferences and the manager arranges one or two exploratory meetings.

Central matching of needs to appropriate coaches. The register of the pool is kept centrally. The list is monitored to identify which coaches have current availability and what recent feedback there has been on their coaching. Then:

- The individual's specific development needs and learning preferences are identified by their line manager or local HR resource.
- The coaching manager identifies two or three suitable coaches based on what they have been told of the individual's needs and their knowledge of the pool.
- The individual is provided with information about one or two suitable coaches, which they either select from or ask to have introductory meetings with both.
- The individual has exploratory meetings.
- The individual (and possibly coach) notifies the coaching manager of their choice.
- The coaching manager informs the coach and ensures the necessary contractual arrangements.
- The individual has first contracting meeting with the selected coach.

A number of the larger organizations I studied had chosen to outsource the management of their external pool of coaches and the coaching matching process. This can provide efficiency savings and access to a wider pool of coaches, but can result in the coaching being less embedded within the organization.

Three- or four-way contracting. I have written extensively about the danger of coaching becoming too focused on the individual client and under-serving the organizational client (Hawkins, 2006, 2008, 2010; Hawkins and Smith, 2006). At worst this can deteriorate into a 'drama triangle' (Karpman, 1968), where the coach sees the coachee as a victim, the organization as a persecutor, and themselves as the rescuer. Good executive coaching always maintains a focus on all three clients: the individual, the organization, and the relationship between the two.

One of the major improvements in quality executive coaching in the last ten years is the introduction of three-way contracting. In this process, the coach meets with both the individual client and their line manager, or someone who can represent the organization's interests in benefiting from this coaching relationship. When I coach a chief executive, I normally meet with the chairman of the Board, and when coaching the chairman meet with the senior non-executive director. It is important that this third person does not simply fulfil the role of the sponsor of the individual's development, but also bears responsibility for the organization learning and benefiting from the coaching. Sometimes it is important to have two representatives of the larger organization, both a more senior leader or manager and a senior person from the HR function. This allows the conversation to focus both on development and performance in their current role and also how the coaching can support development for future potential roles within the business. In addition, the HR representative can focus on how the coaching might link to other leadership development initiatives and programmes.

This three- or four-way meeting usually takes place after the first meeting with the individual client, so the individual client can be part of deciding how to get the best value from this meeting. In the three- or four-way contracting meeting, it is important to develop a joint contract that addresses the following questions:

- How will all parties know that this has been a worthwhile investment of time and money?
- What would be different, both in the individual and in the organization, if the coaching was successful?
- What current strengths, skills, and behaviours of the coachee should the coaching build on?
- What developmental and learning needs of the individual should be addressed?
- How will the organization learn and benefit from this coaching?
- How and when will the coaching be reviewed?

It is beneficial if all the parties can meet to review, progress, and update the contract in the light of what has emerged halfway through the coaching, and then again at the end of the coaching process to evaluate what has been achieved.

> The coaching scheme for the UK National Professional Qualification in Headship introduced coaching for all prospective school head teachers. They undertook a pilot study of the use of three-way contracting between the coach, the trainee head, and their line manager. When asked about the value of such meetings, they were overwhelmingly positive, making such statements as 'very worthwhile', 'very much valued', and 'essential not just desirable'. The benefits included the line manager being clearer about the coaching and the overall leadership development and clearer about how they could provide better developmental opportunities and learning for the trainee head. There were also unexpected benefits. One line manager mentioned how the three-way session was 'a valuable session that has enabled us to clarify our understanding and talk seriously about how we work as a leadership team'.

8. Continuous personal and professional development of the coaches including supervision

As mentioned above, the best organizations not only require coaches to be receiving supervision to get on the short list of applicants, but also require that they can demonstrate how supervision is regularly improving the quality of coaching they deliver. A few organizations are now asking all their coaches to have supervision from the same external organization, so that this supervision can ensure:

- the alignment of coaching to the organization's needs;
- all coaches are updated about changes in the organization through the supervisor;
- rapid transfer of best practice;
- feedback via the supervisor of emerging themes, while maintaining confidentiality;
- emerging recommendations on ways of improving the coaching process.

> The NHS Institute for Innovation and Improvement provide group supervision for both their external panel of individual coaches and separately for their external panel of board and team coaches. This is carried out on two full days each year for each group, and combines group supervision with continuous professional development (CPD) for the coaches. This development focuses on the latest advances in coaching practice as well as updates on what is happening in the Health Service organizationally and its wider context. Sue Mortlock, who leads the National Health Service Institute coaching provision, stated how these supervision and CPD days made a significant difference to the contribution of the coaching resource and built a committed community of external coaching providers.

9. Harvesting the organizational learning

At the end of each coaching relationship, the coaching manager should obtain written feedback from both the coach and the coachee – and, if possible, the line manager – on progress made. It is possible to maximize the learning of all parties if this feedback is openly shared across all parties. This feedback can be used in a number of ways:

- to help the coachee explore how to continue their learning and development after the coaching has ended and link the development from their coaching to other forms of learning on and off the job;
- to enable the coach to identify what has been most and least successful and how they can increase their added value to other clients in this particular organization and beyond;
- to enable the line manager to continue to support and develop the coachee;

- to enable the coaching service to continue to develop its own service and to provide data that can be used anonymously in the on-going evaluation of coaching in the organization (see Chapter 13 on evaluation);
- for themes concerning organization patterns, issues, and learning to be drawn out (while preserving confidentiality) to support the harvesting of the organizational learning (see Chapter 7).

In Chapter 7, I show how organizational learning can be derived from the many individual coaching engagements that an organization may undertake and it is important that those employing external coaches attend to how they manage such processes.

Conclusion

To achieve real value from your external coaches requires the following: a clear coaching policy that defines the nature of coaching and how it works and benefits the organization; a profiling and selection process for ensuring that the organization has the coaches of the right quality and fit; a process for matching coaches and clients; three-way contracting; and processes for inducting, supervising, updating, and developing your selected coaches, as well as harvesting the organizational learning with and from the coaches.

In the next chapter, I look again at some of these issues in relation to developing a community of internal coaches, as well as the differential benefits of using internal and external coaches. Where organizations use both internal and external coaches, it is important that learning is enabled across these two communities.

5 Step 2: Developing the internal coaching and mentoring capacity

Introduction

Recently, CIPD (2009) found that over 90 per cent of organizations reported using coaching, and that 63 per cent delivered this internally by line managers supported by trained internal coaches. Alison Maxwell (2011) distinguishes between four types of internal coaching:

- *Manager as coach* – 'a line manager who draws on a coaching mind-set and coaching skill set' (this is explored in detail in Chapter 9).
- *Crisis intervention* – 'here an employee may present to their line manager (or HR) with an issue that may have erupted as some form of personal crisis, e.g. bereavement, alcoholism, drug abuse, depression or relationship issue'. This I believe is more aptly termed 'counselling at work'.
- *Coach as change agent* – 'individuals working in a change capacity, perhaps on a strategic initiative lasting a number of months or years'. This is similar to project team coaching as described by Hawkins (2011a).
- *Developmental coaching* – an individual who offers developmental or remedial coaching to employees of the same organization, as a recognized part of their job description.

In this chapter, I focus on the last of these forms of internal coaching, which is by far the most common. As Maxwell shows, this is different from giving all line managers and leaders the skills to coach their own staff, which I address in Chapter 9. However, some organizations have created their own internal coaching resource beginning with coach training for line managers. Then, when they have completed their coach training, some of the managers volunteer for further coach development and supervision, and agree to allot two or three hours a week to coaching managers from different parts of the organization.

Other organizations have developed internal coaching after discovering that the number of managers for whom coaching would be beneficial far exceeds the resources the organization has for external coaching. A number of organizations that I interviewed reported that having developed an internal coaching community, they discovered other organizational and economic benefits, including:

- those who undertook coach training and coached managers from other parts of the organization became better managers and leaders in their own teams and departments;
- the coaches became more aware of the organization as a whole and how the various divisions and departments connected;
- they found their on-going connection with other internal coaches across the organization a useful network that supported them in their work.

The journey towards creating, building, and maintaining a quality community of internal coaches requires investment, long-term commitment and support, and careful planning. It should not be undertaken lightly.

The comparative benefits of individual and external coaches

For most organizations, there is a need to have both internal and external coaching as part of creating a strong coaching resource, as each has its own benefits. In research carried out in 2010–2011, the Institute of Leadership and Management (Pardey, 2011) found that 78 per cent of the 250 organizations that responded used coaching. Of these, 83 per cent used internal coaches (both line managers and specialists) and 65 per cent used external coaches, with many using both. Three-quarters of those responding used external coaches for different things from the internal coaches, 53 per cent saying they reserved external coaching for the more senior executives. Table 5.1 shows how to use the two resources in your organization.

A number of writers have articulated some of the particular challenges internal coaches face in their work (Strumpf, 2002; Corporate Research Forum, 2006; St. John-Brooks, 2010; Maxwell, 2011). These include:

- the concerns of the coachee regarding trust and confidentiality, particularly where the coach is part of HR;
- coaches feeling inhibited in providing frank feedback, especially to more senior staff;

Table 5.1 Advantages of internal and external coaches

Advantages of internal coaches	Advantages of external coaches
More aware of the organization's culture and what works and doesn't work	Fresh external perspective, more able to see the taken-for-granted culture and assumptions than those who are part of the organization
Can make links with other work opportunities in the organization	Independent and can ensure greater impartiality and confidentiality
Can empathize with some of the organizational difficulties	Less likely to collude
Will be more aware of other learning and development initiatives in the organization	Will be able to bring awareness of best practice from a wider range of organizations
Can often provide coaching more economically for a wider range of managers	More acceptable for senior executives who would find it difficult to be coached internally for personal and political reasons

- managing internal boundaries, both in the coaching and supervision, where there may be other connections with the coachee;
- the potential for divided and/or conflicting loyalties.

As we shall see in the rest of this chapter and the BBC case study, all of these can be addressed by an organization that is willing to invest in the appropriate training, development, and supervision of internal coaches, as well as set up the requisite boundaries.

Internal coaches and internal mentors

A number of the organizations I interviewed had developed not only an internal coaching network, but also actively supported processes of internal mentors.

The Chartered Institute of Personnel and Development (CIPD) usefully explored the differences between coaching and mentoring. They veered away from too rigid a definition and instead looked at differences between mentoring and coaching by comparing and contrasting the focus and types of activities that characterize them, as shown in Table 5.2 (CIPD, 2004).

The key elements that occur regularly in Table 5.2 shape the CIPD (2004) definition of 'mentoring' as:

- entailing broader ranging, longer term conversations;
- dictated more by the mentee's needs for future career development than specific issues in present job;

Table 5.2 Differences between mentoring and coaching

Mentoring	Coaching
On-going relationships that can last for a long time	Relationships generally have a set duration
Can be more informal and meetings can take place as and when the mentee needs some advice, guidance or support	Generally more structured in nature and meetings are scheduled on a regular basis
More long-term and takes a broader view of the person	Short-term (sometimes time-bounded) and focused on specific development areas/issues
Mentor is usually more experienced than the mentee; often a senior member of the organization who can pass on knowledge and experience and open doors to out-of-reach opportunities	Coaching is generally not performed on the basis that the coach needs to have direct experience of their client's formal occupational role, unless the coaching is specific and skills focused
Focus is on career and personal development	Focus is generally on development/issues at work
Agenda is set by the mentee, with the mentor providing support and guidance to prepare them for future roles	The agenda focuses on achieving immediate specific goals
Mentoring revolves more around developing the mentee professionally	Coaching revolves more around specific development areas/issues

- the mentor using their industry/sector experience to guide the mentee's professional development.

This means that the role is less about creating precise and focused behaviour change and more about helping the mentee to construct a relevant larger picture that will animate their career choices in the future.

In some of the professional service firms I interviewed, it was senior partners who mentored younger staff who were identified as potential future partners. Other firms also used mentoring for newly appointed partners.

> Peninah Thomson and others (Thomson and Graham, 2005) developed the FTSE 100 Cross-Company Mentoring Programme, in which 45 leading UK companies currently participate. The mentoring is for a senior female leader in each company, nominated by her chairman as having the potential to become a board member, and who is mentored by the chairman of another FTSE 100 company to avoid any potential conflict of interest. This programme has proved very successful. Thirty-nine women have completed it to date, with an additional thirty-five currently taking part. Fifteen have been appointed to the executive committee or

main board of their own FTSE company. Nine have been appointed to a non-executive director position in a FTSE company. Fifteen have been promoted within their own company or have moved to another company to gain promotion. Three women have been named as chief executive of a FTSE 250 or other company. There has been formative learning not only for the female mentees but also for the chairmen, who are predominately male. Twelve countries have started to introduce their version of this programme to support more women obtaining positions on the Board (Thomson and Lloyd, 2011).

Stages in forming, building, and maintaining an internal coaching community

In my interviews with organizations that have successfully established internal coaching communities, I found many different approaches. However, in reflecting on their different stories, I discovered there were some discernible stages that most, but not all, had negotiated. There were also additional steps that some organizations wished, in retrospect, they had undertaken. From this study, I have created the following map of the most useful stages.

1. Strategic planning

Similar to forming an external panel of coaches, it is important that before developing an internal coaching community, a coaching strategy and policy are in place (see Chapter 4). In addition to what is necessary for establishing an external pool of coaches, it is important that the coaching policy distinguishes when it is appropriate to use internal and when appropriate to use external coaches.

Liz Macann, who heads up coaching at the BBC, writes:

> The reasons for asking for an external coach are typically:
>
> - the coachee is a senior person;
> - confidentiality (for example, high-profile person or issue);
> - desire to draw on coach's experience (in a coach/mentor type role); for example, real exploration about running a broadcasting organization, someone saturated in the industry can draw on knowledge; commercial expertise.

The BBC also requires external coaching to be funded by the business's own budgets, while internal coaching is centrally funded. This requires managers to think twice before considering an external coach.

In addition, the coaching strategy should consider when to use internal or external coaches and when mentoring might be more appropriate. There is also a fundamental choice to be made. Many organizations such as the BBC chose to develop a cadre of individuals drawn from all parts of the organization with different functional backgrounds, who were interested in doing coaching, alongside their full-time role. Other organizations such as Pricewaterhouse-Coopers and KPMG decided they would instead develop a specialized full-time team of highly trained coaches, who could bring the quality of coaching of many external coaches, while having a much greater understanding of the business context and strategic direction, being more flexible regarding time and less expensive. The BBC now has a mixed model of a few full-time coaches and a large pool of part-time coaches (see the case study at the end of the chapter).

2. Learning from others

There are many traps and pitfalls in establishing and sustaining an internal coaching community, thus rather than reinvent the wheel and repeat mistakes made by others, it is useful to contact others who have been down the road before you. Professional associations in HR and in coaching can often put you in touch with other organizations that have well-established services. The Association of Professional Executive Coaching and Supervision and the European Mentoring and Coaching Council in the UK have special forums for organizations that provide coaching both internally and externally.

3. Recruiting

It is important before recruiting to decide the key competencies, capabilities, and capacities necessary for effective coaches in your organization. Some of these will be generic to all coaches (Hawkins and Smith, 2006). A good baseline is the eleven competencies developed and used by the International Coaching Federation (ICF, 2011):

- A. Setting the foundation
    1. Meeting ethical guidelines and professional standards
    2. Establishing the coaching agreement
- B. Co-creating the relationship
    3. Establishing trust and intimacy with the client
    4. Coaching presence
- C. Communicating effectively
    5. Active listening
    6. Powerful questioning
    7. Direct communication

D. Facilitating learning and results
   8. Creating awareness
   9. Designing actions
   10. Planning and goal setting
   11. Managing progress and accountability

Other competencies and qualities will be specific to your organization and its current challenges. For example, you may want your coaches to be role models for the company's values, or to be individuals likely to be promoted into a leadership role in the near future. It is also important that you check they have the resource and permission, from their senior managers, to devote time not only to complete the training but be available as a coach outside their own department.

A typical assessment form for internal coaches might combine the information in Table 5.3 with a ranking against the basic competencies listed above.

Table 5.3 Internal coach assessment form

Area	1. Desired requirement	2. Applicant's score	3. Weighting of element	Weighted score (2 × 3)
Length of time in the company				
Good people management scores on performance review				
Manager supports their application				
Manager agrees to them having the time both to do the coaching training and the coaching				
Previous coaching experience as coach or client				
Coach training, if any				
Psychological training or experience				
Qualities and personal attributes necessary to role model the internal values				
Relevant wider business experience				
Business qualifications				
Ability to handle ethical dilemmas				

4. Training

Having selected the potential coaches, it is important to provide them with a coach training, geared to the specific needs of the organization. The training needs to cover:

- the coaching strategy – and the part that coaching plays in helping the organization achieve its mission, business strategy, organizational development plans, leadership and talent development plans;
- the specific coaching policy for the organization;
- how coaching is managed;
- the do's and don'ts of coaching in this organization;
- some basic definitions of coaching and how it is different from counselling, mentoring, managing, etc.;
- some basic coaching models such as CLEAR (Hawkins and Smith, 2006) or GROW (Whitmore, 2002);
- all the basic skills of coaching as listed above, with the opportunity to learn them experientially, through practice work coaching each other in threes (coach, client, observer) with structured feedback. It is important that these practice coaching sessions use real current issues, as this maximizes the learning in all three roles, thus they are not role play but 'real play' (Hawkins and Smith, 2006);
- having presentations, followed by questions and dialogue, from individuals already coaching and those who have received coaching, sharing their experience of what worked, what did not work, and the learning they have had.

Some companies have chosen to have their internal coach training accredited, so that their coaches have a recognized qualification or accreditation which is portable and which they can build upon. Two of the major organizations that accredit such training are the Institute for Leadership and Management and the European Mentoring and Coaching Council.

5. Targeting the coach provision

Very few organizations will be able to develop and sustain a large enough coaching community to provide coaching for everyone. Therefore, it is important for organizations to decide where they are going to best utilize their limited coaching resource. There are many ways of focusing, including:

(a) Prioritizing those who are in transition to more senior roles. This might be promotion to:

- a first leadership role, leading a team or a division;
- a move from a functional manager to a corporate role;
- leading a large international account team;
- becoming a partner, or taking on a corporate leadership role;
- joining the board;
- taking on a specific challenge – such as leading a cross-functional change team, or managing a merger or an acquisition.

(b) Other companies have linked their coaching provision to those chosen to attend a leadership or senior management programme, with the coaching helping the individual to ensure they can link the learning on the programme with the challenges faced at work.

(c) Others have ensured that the coaching is linked to those who are identified in their talent management processes to have the capability to progress to a more senior leadership role, and the coaching is focused on ensuring that the individual is helped to use their current challenges to learn the skills and develop the qualities and behaviours necessary for future roles.

Based on the case study at the end of this chapter you will see that the BBC has focused on approaches (a) and (b). In contrast, HSBC chose approach (c) as they wanted to build for the long term a much better leadership talent pipeline. Ernst and Young in the UK focused on a specialized version of (a) as they realized that to grow the business they needed to bring in a number of highly skilled direct entry partners, who were already successful in the market, from other professional services firms. Traditionally, it had taken 18 months for a direct entry partner to negotiate the learning curve of finding ways of being successful in their new organization, and they wanted coaching to dramatically accelerate this process.

6. Matching client and coach

The process of matching client and coach starts with a simple process of ascertaining the needs of the individual coaching client, which can be undertaken by the client's line manager, the local HR manager or by the individual client themselves. Some organizations have developed a simple on-line pro-forma that addresses the following:

- name;
- role;
- length of time in current role;
- future role aspirations;
- reason for wanting coaching;

- skills, behaviours, and qualities you would like to develop through the coaching;
- describe how you learn best;
- describe the qualities and approach you would want in a coach;
- any specific preferences in terms of language requirement, age, gender or experience.

A few organizations have out-sourced the coach matching service to an external third party, but this is less common than out-sourcing the external coach matching. Others have used an e-enabled system whereby coaches' biographies and background are on line and employees can contact them directly via this system.

7. Supervision and continuous personal and professional development for the coaches

The initial training mentioned above will only provide the foundation for the learning journey in becoming an effective coach. The most important learning happens as the apprentice coach starts to practise with their first clients. Some organizations start new coaches on practice volunteer clients, before they take on more senior clients with more pressing and business-critical issues. Either way it is essential that the on-going learning is supported as much as the initial training. Supervision has a critical role to play in this continuing personal and professional development of the coach (see Chapter 12). In 2006, when I jointly carried out research on coaching supervision for the CIPD (Hawkins and Schwenk, 2006), 88 per cent of the 125 organizations that completed the questionnaire thought that supervision was essential for all coaches, but only 23 per cent provided supervision for their internal or external coaches. This has changed significantly in the last five years, but still has some way to go. When organizations do provide supervision, it is often through employing an external supervisor or an organization that provides coaching supervisors. A few organizations such as the BBC (see case study) and the National Health Service (through the National Health Service Institute for Innovation and Improvement) train their own internal supervisors.

Good practice suggests that the new supervisor should have one hour of supervision for every 10 hours of coaching, whereas an experienced coach should have one hour of supervision for every 35 hours of coaching (Hawkins and Smith, 2006). Often a mixture of individual and group supervision is beneficial. The group supervision increases the learning the coaches get from each other as well as building the community of practice. The individual supervision allows for more in-depth attention to the coach's breadth of clients and their own particular development.

Many of the organizations interviewed also provided regular master classes by internal and external experts on particular aspects of coaching. The organizations reported that these were best when they included an opportunity to explore the application of this approach in their own organization and time to practise it live in the master class. Topics covered included specific methods (transformational coaching, solution focused, NLP, Gestalt, etc.), working with transcultural differences, ethical dilemmas, handling conflict, methods for contracting and reviewing work, and so on.

8. Annual reviews of the service with all members of the service

Despite having done what you can to learn as many lessons as possible from other organizations (see above), all those I interviewed noted how much their coaching service had to learn and adapt as it developed. A number had instituted an annual (or occasionally more frequent) conference for everyone involved in coaching. Most organizations combined this event with a talk from a senior executive on the strategic challenges for the organization and an update on new changes in the company, its strategy approach, values and organization, and leadership development. Some also brought in a very experienced external coach to provide a master class on a new direction within coaching. Much of the benefit of such an event is to build the community of practice and sustain the enthusiasm and commitment of the volunteer coaches.

The Electricity Supply Board, Ireland's premier electricity utility company, used its recent conference to address the challenge: 'How can we collectively double the value of coaching in our company?' What emerged from this interactive process is addressed in Chapter 7, where I look at different forms of harvesting the learning, to which I also turn now.

9. Harvesting the learning

The collective coaching community may have coaching relationships with a large number of leaders in the organization and once again it is important that organizational learning is garnered from these individual coaching conversations. This involves methods of collecting feedback on all coaching relationships, ideally from both parties. This is similar to what was described in Chapter 4.

In Chapter 7, I show how organizational learning can be derived from the many individual coaching engagements that an organization may undertake. It is important that those managing the internal coaching community attend to the way in which they manage such processes.

10. Evaluation and further development

As well as the evaluation that emerges from the annual conference and other forms of harvesting the learning, most of the organizations I interviewed agreed that it was essential to have an on-going evaluation process in place. This was not only to justify the continuing investment in coaching activities, but also regularly to refine the coaching strategy and process.

There are three main forms of coaching evaluation that can be built into the on-going coaching management process:

1. Each coaching relationship has specific goals for the coaching as part of the initial coaching contract and developed through the three- or four-way coaching contract process and the mid relationship review. Then, at the end of the coaching relationship, data are collected from all three or four parties on how well these goals have been achieved.
2. Every coaching client, coach, and client manager completes feedback forms on the coaching, both at the end of the coaching contract and a further six months later. The second feedback is undertaken because often the benefits of coaching take some time to emerge.
3. An annual audit of the coaching service is carried out, which includes:
   - number of clients seen and a breakdown of different levels and functions;
   - average length of contract;
   - number of coaches active and average number of clients seen;
   - average feedback ratings from clients on the value of the coaching, the coaching relationship, and the coaching service;
   - scores on initial goals achieved by client, coach, and client's manager;
   - success of clients who receive coaching in improving their performance scores and achieving promotion, compared with staff at the same level who did not receive coaching.

The wider issues of evaluation and how it links to wider coaching research and issues around return on investment are considered in Chapter 13.

Coaching across organizations

A number of organizations, particularly in the public sector, have collaborated to provide coaching to each other's organization. An excellent example of this is the West Midland Local Government Association, where coaches and later coach supervisors were trained from across the region's different public sector organizations. A central help register meant that individuals could find a coach provided by another of the participating organizations.

In another region of the UK, the North West Employers combined with their local National Health Service, North West Leadership Academy to provide a joint training for chief executives from across the region. As a condition of doing the training, the chief executives agreed to provide coaching to senior executives from other participating organizations. This joint venture was part of a wider strategy to increase capacity of senior leaders to work across sectors and develop the next generation of leaders and chief executives. In her evaluation report, Lynn Scott found that the programme had not only been successful in developing the participants' coaching skills, but had also built better supportive and collaborative working across the region. Several participants also reported how they were now attempting to create a coaching culture in their organization.

The following BBC case study was contributed by Liz Macann, Head of Coaching at the corporation.

Case study: The BBC

History of coaching at the BBC
The programme originated in Greg Dyke's time as Director General. He encouraged the staff to make things happen rather than wait to be told what to do. This encouraged Liz Macann to follow her passion to bring coaching to the BBC. There had been some coaching for the very top level. Training and Development put out an offer of internal coaching via free pilots and was inundated. The beginning was not top-down, but people-up.

What is understood by coaching?
The in-house coaching service trains and manages a process to link line managers working as executive coaches to coachees from other parts of the organization. The impact on the management skills of those trained as coaches is believed to be significant, but this is treated as an added ancillary benefit rather than the aim of the BBC approach.

There is also a 'Coaching Skills for Managers' course to help managers use coaching skills in managing their people. This is run with cohorts of twelve managers over two modules with practical learning back at work in between. The programmes are a combination of input, practice, observation, and feedback.

Overall objectives for coaching
Coaching at the BBC is a leadership development process, offering support and development for leaders to develop their self-responsibility and self-awareness. Its aims are to:

- support managers in times of change and when changing role;
- develop leadership capability;
- develop the potential of identified talent.

Developing internal coaching resources
The coaching programmes use line managers as coaches. There are now seventy coaches, with twelve more being developed. All coaches have 'day' jobs and get no extra pay for coaching.

Qualifying to be a coach within the organization involves a rigorous selection (limited to twenty-four places a year) and development process as well as a process of continuing development while they are coaching.

Most of those who apply have received coaching themselves and this had given them the motivation to be involved:

> "I was on the leadership programme with a coach. It was so powerful, one of the most powerful things I took away that gelled the learning of the week. It interested me and I persuaded the BBC to let me do some more."

The procedure to apply starts with filling in an application form, where the prospective coach is encouraged to think about their skills in terms of their interest in people, capacity for detachment, listening, and their understanding of what coaching is trying to achieve. Candidates are shortlisted by the senior staff in the coaching service. Applicants must be supported by their line manager and meet the stipulated criteria to be shortlisted.

The final stage is an interview with members of the coaching service to explore motivation, organizational credibility, personal presence, and determine if they have the time to do it. Successful applicants are then offered a place on the Coaching Foundations Course (CFC), which is accredited by the European Mentoring and Coaching Council (EMCC) and the International Coaching Federation (ICF). Participants attend the course, which is run by three tutors (two internal and one external), in cohorts of twelve.

The programme is structured around the five coaching competencies used at the BBC:

- organization (including session planning, note taking, planning and logistics of session, and so on);
- analytical skills (during the session – understanding the 'story', choice of interventions, and so on);
- self-awareness (recognizing what they are doing well and the impact they are having);
- building relationships (establishing a trusting, safe, yet challenging, confidential space);
- communication skills (listening and questioning);
- and underpinned by the ICF's eleven competencies.

Key elements of the course include:

- three modules, with taught sessions in the morning and practicals in the

afternoon; in the afternoon, the participants undertake some coaching with one another and give each other feedback, observed by a tutor;
- skills work between the modules, supported by mentors;
- two practice clients – people of at least middle-manager level with real issue(s) to work on, who have agreed to be coached by them for the duration of the training programme and to provide evaluation;
- a coach mentor (a coach and graduate of an earlier programme) to support them through the development process;
- evaluation of their competence each day of each module (how the tutors are experiencing them) and in practice; and
- a final assessment, including: a final observed session on the last day working with the client with a genuine issue; learning journal; client evaluation forms; mentor reports and experience of tutors (based on observation of competencies, their 'signature presence', and whether or not the tutors feel that they would enjoy being coached by this person (not all of them have to say yes, but at least one of them needs to).

When a coach has completed the programme and joined the service, they stop working with their mentor and are assigned a supervisor, who they see quarterly.

> With your supervisor you can focus on one thing, in the group you can learn from others, their different experiences, get help for things you're working on.
> After I finished training I've had supervision, my learning has continued constantly, it has been brilliant for me, thinking out loud, I get to think the sessions through – it's like coaching itself. Training has the tools and in supervision I get reminded of them.

Sharing learning across the coaching community
Every quarter, internal coaches attend shared learning groups (10–12 coaches). These sessions include group supervision and exchanging models and ideas. Twice a year they all get together (summer and Christmas) and have an interesting speaker from the world of coaching, some networking time, and lunch. Some informal sub-groups have also formed and meet on a regular basis. Both the group and the individual supervision are highly valued by the coaches.

The Standard Executive Coaching Programme
Liz Macann allocates coaches based on an understanding of the coach's level of coaching capability (in terms of seniority of coachee) and coach preferences. Typically, coaches will not coach someone more senior than themselves until they have gained a significant amount of experience. Thirty of the existing coaches, as well as the coach managers, do senior coaching, having been specially selected for this.

The coachee is not given a choice of coach. One rule of the allocation process is that coaches cannot coach within their own BBC division or functional specialty.

A key consideration for the coaches is the possible prior knowledge they may have of their coachee's situation and, in particular, people they work with, for example the coachee's line manager. As they become more senior, it becomes inevitable that they know people in the organization with whom their coachee is interacting. The coaches I spoke to, explained that they have needed to listen to the level of distraction they experience when a name gets mentioned that they know. They explained that they have to make a split-second judgement about whether the distraction is likely to be something that needs to be brought up and made transparent to the coachee or not. This is apparently typical of the sorts of issues the coaches discuss in their regular shared learning meetings.

The coachee generates objectives for the coaching programme and works with the coach to generate measures, which includes the following consideration: 'What will your line manager or division have gained from this work?'

A coaching programme includes an initial objective-setting meeting with the coach, a three-way meeting with coach, coachee and line manager, and then five coaching sessions (three to four weeks apart). The first three-way meeting is now mandatory and coaches are asked not to continue until this has happened after many experiences of getting to four sessions and without having a conversation with the manager. In some cases, coaches used to have a one-to-one conversation with the manager when their coachee was not present. However, this created feelings of tension and anxiety in the coachees about what had been said, so all of these conversations are now three-way. A follow-up post-coaching meeting with the manager also takes place.

Line managers fit coaching into their work schedule in a way that suits them, but this can raise conflicts. Finding times that work for both parties is a difficulty most coaches face, but it seems this turns out to be more of an issue for coachees.

Occasionally, either for reasons of conflict of interest or chemistry, a coachee is returned to the service to be reallocated to a new coach.

The service ran 500 coaching programmes in 2010. Duration varies by seniority and programme; for the standard service, more junior managers will have 10 hours over six months, rising to 20 hours over twelve months for the most senior staff.

The coaching takes place face to face for UK-based staff, while some staff in other locations are coached by phone.

First 100 days: People in Transition Programme
This is a specific, intensive coaching programme for people who are joining the organization, changing role (for example, through promotion) or changing department/division. Based on research that says you have 90 days to make an

impact in a new role or organization, people need to join the programme within three weeks of their change of role. It is available for managers that have been nominated by their line managers.

In this programme, the role of the coach is to act as a partner to the coachee for 100 days. In the first month they will meet once a week face to face, with regular contact by phone and email. For the rest of the 100 days they can meet as regularly as they agree, up to a limit of ten hours.

BBC leadership development programmes
The BBC used to offer a suite of leadership development programmes (for team leaders, middle managers, and senior managers). In these programmes coaching was offered to a limited extent to team leaders, middle managers had four coaching sessions, and senior managers had six sessions with a BBC coach. The coaching was driven by 360-degree feedback. A new leadership programme is currently being designed, which will include coaching linking into the business by including the line manager in determining success measures. It will be structured as per the Executive Coaching Programme – with seven sessions, including the initial and three-way contracting sessions.

External coaches
External coaches are funded by the divisions from their own budgets. The coaching function compiled a list of preferred suppliers, which contains twenty-five individuals and organizations. Each organization can field a maximum of three named coaches. The list is now held by procurement rather than the Network to avoid potential conflict in selecting external and internal coaches. In external coaches they look for top qualifications and a 'signature presence' that will work in the corporation. This includes: integrity, authenticity, and an ability to connect with the person.

The reasons for asking for an external coach are typically:

- the coachee is a very senior person;
- confidentiality (for example, high-profile person or issue);
- desire to draw on coach's experience (in a coach/mentor type role); for example, real exploration about running a big organization to draw on specific knowledge and commercial expertise.

Evaluation
The BBC runs an overall evaluation process every year. Individual coaching programmes are evaluated as follows:

- three-way review session;
- client evaluation forms are sent to the coachee at the end of the programme and returned to head office;
- a copy of the evaluation form goes to the coach and their supervisor, who then explore the messages in the evaluation.

Typically, clients are asked:

- to describe their experience;
- to provide feedback on their coach's style;
- what are the most and least effective sessions;
- how they have benefited;
- what they do differently as a result;
- what others will notice them doing differently;
- to make suggestions for improvement;
- if they would recommend the programme to others.

The BBC has also carried out various qualitative studies. In one recent research sample, coachees identified that being 'forced' to take time to think, the challenging questions, and the opportunity to work with an impartial person were all critical to the success of their coaching experience. Here are some typical responses:

> Huge impact on my style as a manager, for example my understanding of how different people are and how my own emotional reactions can be understood and how I can work with them, how I am directive and the true meaning of delegation . . . I now coach my staff and they say they feel I am very supportive.
>
> There's been a total change in the way I run my team. It's smoother, they have autonomy, they love it, between us we produce more, with less grief, and I get fewer questions about how they should do things, with less tension.

Reflections on the coaching service
The coaching service has achieved a great deal and is regularly approached by organizations both in the UK and internationally for advice on setting up internal coaching services. One of the advantages of working with internal coaches is that coaches can feed back the mood and key issues that staff are grappling with in a totally confidential way without mentioning names. This is fed back through shared learning groups to the lead coaches and from there to senior management. One disadvantage with trying to fit coaching around the day job is guilt. One coach described feeling 'guilty about leaving my team to it when I'm going to workshops and taking time out to coach other people'.

Possible opportunities for the development of BBC coaching
The members of the coaching service are interested in building their reputation within the corporation, ensuring more managers know about the programmes on offer, their benefits and impact. Coaching is publicized through the leadership programmes, where it's an optional part of the programme and

> linked to recruitment for the first 100 days. It is also highlighted in the training bulletin and offered as part of 'learning at work week', as well as having a page in the intranet. Most crucially, HR has taken on board the value of coaching and, going forward, will be the first stop for staff wanting to coach or be coached, allowing the coaching offered to be a strategic intervention.

Conclusion

In the last five years there has been a major growth in the number of organizations developing their internal coaching communities. This process is now accelerating, partly driven by the economic crisis as all organizations are looking at every item of their costs and identifying greater value for money. Most organizations are continuing to invest more in their coaching provision (CIPD, 2009), as they realize that it is a cost-effective element of developing and retaining their best talent. However, many are reducing their investment on external coaches and investing more in their internal coach training, development, and supervision.

6 Step 3: The organization's leaders actively support coaching endeavours and align these endeavours to the organizational culture change

Introduction

This chapter is directed in particular at chief executives and their fellow directors and senior executives, including the HR director, for the senior leadership are critical players in making the step change from being an organization that provides coaching to an organization that has a coaching culture.

Once an organization has set up its pool of external coaches and formed its internal coaching (and mentoring) community, it has done a lot of the groundwork in laying the foundations of a coaching culture by putting in place some of the key inputs. However, if it stops at this point, it will have provided a lot of the expensive inputs, but is unlikely to harvest the outputs and the beneficial outcomes. At this stage, the organization may have many managers receiving coaching or mentoring, but without support this will not translate into managers and leaders coaching their own staff, and becoming coach leaders. It is helpful for the chief executive to make positive oral and written communications about the importance of coaching, and the difference it can make for the organization. However, actions always speak louder than words and it will have more impact if the chief executive also talks positively about their own experience of coaching and what they learnt and developed from coaching. The chief executive will have even more influence on changing the culture if they and their fellow senior leaders start to use a more 'coaching style' of engaging all staff.

At this point, the organization needs to build on the foundation of managing its coaching inputs by developing a coaching style in the leadership. This is the stage where coaching and the wider aspects of culture change need to be connected (see Chapter 3). The change in organizational culture starts with the leadership culture, for 'leaders create the organizational culture that they behave' (Hawkins and Wright, 2009: 18)

Leading the change in the leadership culture: from 'command and control' to 'coaching leadership'

Obolensky (2010) shows how leadership has had to change as organizations have become more complex and global, and the environment they operate in faster changing, more unpredictable, and more interconnected. The dominant leadership style of the mid-twentieth century of 'command and control' is no longer fit for purpose. Such a leadership culture is over-reliant on a few leaders at the top of the organization, who can never see the complexities of the whole system. It also fails to utilize the intelligence and collective knowledge that reside in other parts of the system. With the changing social values mentioned in Chapter 1, 'command and control' leaders can no longer expect a deferential workforce.

Arguably, such a culture was also less effective in the past than the hagiographic biographies of great leaders would suggest. Indeed, Tolstoy pointed out, in his great novel *War and Peace*, that turning points in history are due less to the decisions of heroic leaders, and more to complex systemic currents, including the dynamic culture of the mass of people involved. At the Battle of Borodino, which became one of the turning points of the Napoleonic wars against Russia, many historians had attributed the failure of the French to Napoleon having a bad cold, due to his batman leaving his boots out in the rain! Tolstoy points out that Napoleon was two miles from the action, which, due to the mist, he had no way of seeing. By the time news of the battle reached him by horseback, and his orders relayed back to the men at the front line, those orders had been overtaken by subsequent action. This may have been 200 years ago, but often I meet senior executives who are similarly placed to Napoleon and still try and act as if they are generals who are in charge and know what is happening!

There are many studies and books on the leadership that is required in the complex, fast changing, unpredictable, and globally interconnected world we now live in. These argue that leaders need to be transformational (Tichy and Cohen, 2002), emotionally intelligent (Goleman, 1996, 1998), authentic (George, 2003), ethical (Tichey and McGill, 2003), resonant and compassionate (Boyatzis and McKee, 2005), agile and adaptive (Obolensky, 2010), systemic (Wheatley, 2002; Stacey, 2010), and focused on sustainability (Goleman, 2009; Marshall et al., 2011). That is quite a demanding set of skills!

Obolensky (2010) tries to integrate these attributes and show how the leaders of complex-adaptive organizations of today's world need to combine the Yin of soft principles and the Yang of hard principles (see Table 6.1). Obolensky goes on to show how the adaptive leader is fundamentally different from the technical expert leader in their responses (see Table 6.2).

One of the key skills that all leaders need is the ability to get the best performance and on-going development from the people they lead. This

Table 6.1 The Yin and Yang of complex-adaptive organizations

'Soft' principles – the Yin		'Hard' principles – the Yang
Underlying organizational purpose: the implicit raison d'être, which motivates and unites people	vs.	**Clear individual objectives:** each person knows what he or she is trying to achieve and why, and there is an element of self-setting
People's skill/will: people have the skill to do their job and they are motivated, which allows development	vs.	**Clear boundaries:** these lay down what people are enabled to do or not, and where they should operate
Tolerance to ambiguity: things look a bit chaotic and there is a degree of tolerance to such ambiguity	vs.	**Unambiguous feedback:** there are clear measures that enable people to see how they are doing at any point in time
Freedom to act: individuals have complete discretion regarding how they go about doing jobs/achieving objectives	vs.	**Few simple rules:** there are a few clear rules that lay down how people operate and the key principles they must follow

Table 6.2 Responses of adaptive versus technical leaders

Leadership challenges	Technical leadership response	Adaptive leadership response
Direction	Define problems and find solution	Identify the adaptive challenge and frame key questions
Protection	Shield the organization from external threats	Let the organization feel the pressure within a range it can stand
Orientation	Clarify roles and responsibilities	Challenge current roles and resist defining new roles too quickly
Managing conflict	Restore order	Expose conflict or let it emerge
Shaping norms	Maintain norms	Challenge unproductive norms

requires them not only to have some core coaching skills, but also a coaching style of leadership. The key attributes of a coaching style of leader are as follows:

- They are constantly curious about how employees at all levels as well as the complete range of stakeholders perceive the organization and are interested in their ideas about how things could be improved.
- They establish rapport with a wide range of employees and stakeholders through their ability to listen both actively and empathically, so people feel that they not only understand what has been said, but also understand how the person saying it feels.

- They ask powerful questions that encourage everyone to think differently and they challenge the status quo.
- They use a range of ways to engage people – not just using *advocacy* of the mission, strategy, and what needs to be done but also: *inquiry* – engaging others in deciding how to improve products and processes; *illustrating* – with stories, images, metaphors and pictures, what is already happening that is successful and what is being achieved by others outside the organization; and *framing and reframing* – providing different perspectives and frames through which people can see what is happening through a different lens (Torbert, 2004).
- They engage people at all four levels of engagement (Hawkins and Smith, 2006): (i) data and information, (ii) behaviours, (iii) feelings, and (iv) mindsets and assumptions.
- They can create an impactful shift live in the room, in the way other people are thinking and feeling (Hawkins and Smith, 2010).

The coaching leader needs to be seen to be taking the lead in supporting the move to a coaching culture, not just in their active support of the various coaching activities and in their communications, but also in their behaviours. In the very effective British Airways culture change process in the 1980s, Colin Marshall, the then current chief executive, went to every cohort of their 'Putting People First' leadership programmes, not to preach about the importance of leaders who listen or who coach, but for he himself to listen to the ideas the participants had come up with for radically improving the culture and performance of the business. He would try to take at least one proposal from each programme and conspicuously support it happening in the business, thus role-modelling being a coaching style leader. Actions always speak much louder than words.

A number of the organizations I interviewed had built a coaching style of leadership and coaching skills into the leadership framework for their organization, which informed both leadership selection and all leadership development activities. Thames Valley Police Force reported that their new leadership framework, which included leaders having a coaching style, set the tone for a new style of leadership.

As well as role-modelling a coaching approach, senior leaders can actively support the development of a coaching culture by:

- publicly talking about the benefit they have received from coaching and sharing their learning and development process. None of us are too important or successful to not undertake further learning or experience failures we can learn from;
- being seen to be curious and learning in team meetings, 'town hall' staff engagements, meetings with stakeholders, and other public events;

- having regular dialogues with the coaching communities of internal and external coaches, not just to share with them the current challenges, strategy, and strategic change initiatives of the organization, but to listen to what they are discovering through the many coaching conversations about the current climate in the organization, the cultural patterns, and the enablers and blockers to the organization moving forward most effectively. Having done that, the coaching leader can then explore both what the leadership and the coaching community can best do to address the challenges and build on the strengths, thus turning the coaching community into a valued partner in the development of the organization.

Jack Welch, the chief executive who turned around the performance of General Electric, moved his style of leading from phase one, where he radically restructured and refocused the business and was known as 'Neutron Jack', to phase two, where he spent 25 per cent of his time on coaching and developing the leaders right across the business. He realized that great leaders do not just fight a heroic battle to turn around the short-term business performance, but that 'great leaders create leaders' – and shift the leadership culture to one that is constantly learning and developing (Welch, 2001).

Building coaching into the content and style of all training programmes

The next important step is to build a coaching approach into all the organization's leadership development programmes.

In Chapter 1, I showed how one of the key factors in the rise of coaching was the move in workplace training and development out of theoretical learning in the classroom to a greater focus on learning-on-the-job and addressing complex current challenges. Coaching plays a critical role in this applied learning approach. Most current leadership development programmes either use individual coaching or coaching approaches in syndicate group learning, action learning sets or coaching practicum groups.

Syndicate learning, action learning, and 'reflecting teams'

Some of the origins of this facilitated rather than teaching approach to learning was pioneered by Reg Revans in action learning (Pedler, 1996; Revans, 1998) and the Henley Business School, which developed 'learning syndicates' on their early senior management training (Belbin, 2004). Learning syndicates of managers, drawn from different roles and organizations, were given real organizational challenges to explore and asked to create ways of addressing them.

Action learning sets encouraged set members to bring their current workplace challenges and the whole group would be facilitated to help explore the issues and enable the 'problem-holder' to arrive at a new course of action. Mike Pedler (1997) defines action learning as:

> Action learning couples the development of people in work organizations with action on their difficult problems . . . [it] makes the task the vehicle for learning and has three main components – people, who accept the responsibility for action on a particular task or issue; problems, or the tasks which are acted on; and the set of six or so colleagues who meet regularly to support and challenge each other to take action and to learn.

In their research on action learning, Pedler et al. (2005) found that the majority (over 65 per cent) of action learning set facilitators agreed with the following core aspects:

- sets of about six people;
- action on real tasks or problems at work;
- tasks/problems are individual rather than collective;
- questioning as the main way to help participants proceed with their tasks/problems;
- facilitators are used;
- tasks/problems are chosen independently by individuals.

Both of these methods, syndicate learning and action learning, can be seen as forms of group coaching (Thornton, 2010; Hawkins, 2011a). Both action learning set facilitators and syndicate facilitators need to undergo training in how to coach the group and enable them to use coaching approaches in how they work with their peer colleagues. Indeed, over the last sixty years action learning has developed a series of protocols that set facilitators can introduce and support the learning set in acquiring and using. These include:

- the principle of shared air-time – everybody gets their equal share of time to bring issues and an equal voice in helping others with their issues;
- active listening;
- avoidance of advice giving and jumping to solutions;
- use of inquiry questions to open up the issue being explored;
- brainstorming ways forward and sharing parallel experiences (but not as solutions);
- helping the issue-holder to arrive at a new way to respond to their issue that they are committed to trying out;

- reviewing what happened when the action was tried out, back at work, at the next meeting.

Another form of experiential group learning process draws on the work of Balint et al. (1966) and his development of reflective practice, originally with doctors. This was adapted by Mary Holland, an external coach from Ireland, to help develop a coaching culture across leaders at the European Commission.

Case study: The European Commission
The European Commission's White Paper on Reform of 2000 highlighted the importance of effective management as crucial to the on-going success of the organization. In particular, it identified the need to raise the standard of management skills across the Commission to ensure more effective performance. As the EU grew larger and more complex, the culture shock of joining the organization was too great for some. This particular problem was highlighted after enlargement in 1995 with the admission of Sweden, Finland, and Austria. Many senior managers did not adapt to the very bureaucratic and political culture of working long hours into the evening and they left in large numbers. The organization wished to introduce a system more compatible with the principles of meritocracy rather than political sponsorship and seniority. Furthermore, there was a concern about the lack of women managers and leaders, as well as the cross-cultural skills of their managers.

The Management Training Programme was designed to optimize the management and leadership potential of Heads of Unit. It consisted of eight full days of training, with follow-up sessions to reinforce learning and application. This course was compulsory for all Heads of Unit and as a result of using group reflective processes at this initial step, many managers rapidly experienced and understood a coaching style before external coaching was provided. It set the standard and created the pace for the 'unfreezing', the organization's dominant style of management.

There was an organizational need to have a more balanced representation of women and men in management positions, so the managers experienced the gender differences directly by having two facilitators, one man and one woman. This often meant that I was the only woman in the room. Both facilitators also represented cultural diversity by coming from two different nationalities and speaking in both French and English. Multiple projections were sometimes tested and played out and some participants felt challenged by the culturally cognitive dissonance of having a woman in a position of authority working with them.

The Management Training Programme used a collective group coaching process based upon the process developed by Balint (Balint et al., 1966). The process of 'Reflecting Teams', as the group coaching was called, provided a safe place where managers could talk about work relationships with their key staff or stakeholders and explore how they were handling them on a case by case basis.

> Being able to discuss their own real cases gave the managers many opportunities to connect with each other and learn about each other's multicultural managerial expectations. Each group had an experienced coach to role model and manage the process, so the managers could hone their coaching skills by dealing with their real issues. In these early days, the pioneering use of supportive coaching groups was key in creating an understanding of and engagement with a new managerial culture. Group coaching was both very challenging, and all the more impactful because the group was learning by dealing with their current work challenges.
>
> Group coaching was a more effective way of side-stepping resistance to a new culture through changing the pace and the focus and slowing down. With so many different languages and cultures, with participants often not working in their mother tongue and some not even in their preferred second language, it is sometimes hard for some to express themselves. Language is a crucial aspect of coaching, so the group coaching experience may initially create greater anxiety. However, when handled well it allows for the development of a greater appreciation and empathy for the complexity of each others' roles; strategic linking; an appreciation of who owns the problem; new learning and competence through sharing and action follow-through; and a renewed sensitivity to their staff's experience. Certainly, the feedback about the group coaching showed that the managers perceived it to be transformative.

The coaching practicum group

Having worked with both syndicate learning groups and action learning sets, between 1976 and 1995, I began to be interested in creating a form of leadership development that combined the benefits of these learning modalities, with leaders learning the skills of coaching, as well as more effective engagement with peers, staff, and stakeholders. To this end I developed a new approach called 'the coaching practicum group'. Like the action learning set, the coaching practicum comprises a group of five to seven people drawn from different parts of the organization. It is important to create a maximum mix of roles and people in these groups, not only because this has been shown to deliver more effective team learning and functioning (Belbin, 2004), but also because it restricts the likelihood of group members falling into giving advice or trying to solve each others' issues, as they are less likely to know the background or have the technical skills necessary.

The following is an account of the use of practicum groups in Ernst and Young on a leadership programme for all 550 Partners across the UK and Ireland that was jointly authored by Andrew Wright, the Head of Leadership Development in Ernst and Young in the UK and myself, and published in *Strategic HR Review* (Hawkins and Wright, 2009).

Half of the time at the Leadership Foundation event was spent in small learning groups of six partners, facilitated by a senior coach/trainer from Bath Consultancy Group. The partners were selected to ensure there was a maximum mix from different business units, functional specialisms, offices and seniority. This had the double benefit of partners being able to build new networks across the organization, and, more importantly, finding ways of coaching each other to make a difference that relied on skills other than technical or local knowledge. In the learning groups, individual feedback, gathered from both internal and external sources, was shared and combined with specific development challenges. This enabled the group as well as individuals to form goals for the programme.

'Through this time, real situations were brought to life so the partners could experiment with how to deal with challenging work situations. Each partner had a chance to experience being in the following roles:

- A leader in a real relationship situation.
- A coach who needed to create a shift in how the leader was thinking, feeling and acting.
- A shadow coach who had the responsibility for monitoring the coaching process and helping the coach to raise their game.

In transformational coaching the intention is not for the person bringing the issue or case to leave with just new insight or a 'must do action list', but rather to have had a 'felt shift' in the session where they start to think, feel and act differently in relation to what they have brought (Hawkins and Smith, 2006 and 2010). Bath Consultancy Group's research has shown that the chances of learning and change being transferred back into the live situation are much higher when this occurs than when people leave simply with good intentions. All partners left the foundation with a clearer sense of their strengths and development needs and clear commitments about how they were going to develop their leadership and be an active change agent in developing the partnership.

Following the Foundation, the learning groups continued to meet for follow up sessions two or three times over the following six to nine months. In these sessions the partners gave feedback on how their plans to transform the relationships they had explored on the Foundation have progressed and to undertake further coaching rounds on new internal and external leadership relationship challenges.'

Conclusion

The move to a coaching culture can be seen as a key aspect of three other major shifts in organizations:

- the need for organizations to move from sending staff individually on classroom-based training to being a learning organization;
- a move from hierarchical organizations to complex-adaptive organizations;
- the need for leadership to move from a 'command and control' and 'tell and sell' style to one that has a more engagement, dialogical, and coaching style.

At this step on the coaching culture journey, it is important that leaders become actively engaged in supporting the coaching culture – in words, decisions and, most importantly, their own actions and role modelling. Leaders need to follow the great maxim of Mahatma Ghandi:

> Be the change you want to see.

In Chapter 9, I look at how to develop a coaching style (Step 6), not only in the leadership culture of the organization, but as a core aspect and style of how all managers manage. Before we address that though we need to look at how coaching is built into the other aspects of organizational life, such as team functioning, engagement with staff, and informal coaching conversations (Step 4, Chapter 7) and also into the performance management and HR policies of the organization (Step 5, Chapter 8).

7 Step 4: Coaching moves beyond individual formal sessions to team coaching and organizational learning

Introduction

When I asked one senior director how much coaching went on in her organization, she proudly replied:

> I could not possibly tell you as it is no longer something that happens behind closed doors in confidential one to one sessions for *coaching is how we do business in our organization*, with our staff, our colleagues, our customers, our suppliers and all our other stakeholders. It is how we relate.

In Chapter 10, I explore how to use coaching as a way of engaging stakeholders, but in this chapter I look at the journey from coaching being something that is provided for a chosen few in individual confidential sessions, to something that involves everybody. I also explore the journey from individual coaching to coaching being used for teams, team meetings, and organizational events.

At this stage in developing the coaching culture it is also important for organizations to explore how they harvest the learning from the various coaching endeavours and connect coaching back to the strategy and development of the whole organization. By the time the organization has reached this step, it will have clarified which members of staff should receive coaching from external and which from internal coaches and when in a person's career and development this is most appropriate. However, there will also be a shift in the communications about coaching. The new communications will indicate that coaching is not just something that happens for selected individuals, behind closed doors in special confidential meetings, but that coaching is a way of engaging that encourages others to think through their challenges, engage with new perspectives, and together generate new thinking and action, not possible by either party thinking by themselves.

Corridor coaching

In his simple but wise book called *Seeing Systems*, Barry Oshry (1999, 2007) talks about how the first law of organizations is that 'stuff happens'. Every minute of every day we encounter 'stuff' – a phone call, an e-mail, a conversation, a non-response. Oshry then explains the way that our common human response to 'stuff' is to react and to make up a story about the person who has interacted with us (or not, as the case may be). We find it hard to tolerate not knowing, so we make up a story. For instance, we may think that the reason we have not heard back from the other person is that they are cross with us, or they do not care about us or perhaps that we are not worthwhile. Often, the instant stories we make up portray the other as bad, out to get us, or incompetent, and we want to get even with the imaginary person we have created! This is the emotional noise that pollutes all organizational environments.

In his teaching, Oshry shows how we each have the moment by moment choice to go through Door A, where we become reactive and make up stories, or Door B, where we can make a stand to remain in non-reactive relationship and work to sustain partnership. Oshry describes Door A as always open and easy to go through, almost as if it has a suction pump the other side pulling us through. Door B, on the other hand, looks at first like a brick wall, and you yourself have to work hard to create the door to gain entry. However, others can help and this is where 'corridor coaching' can be extremely helpful.

In some organizations we have worked with, we find that it is common for someone to come up to a colleague and say, 'can I have five minutes of your time', which is recognizable code for 'can I have some short informal coaching time to help me manage a relationship where I think I am about to become reactive'.

Oshry has developed a very well-designed organizational simulation that he has refined and developed over many years. In this simulation of a working company, which includes customers, there are twevve-minute days, followed by individual reflection time and then 'time-out of time' when the whole system can listen to what is being experienced in other parts of the system, before returning to the next twelve-minute day.

With my colleagues at Bath Consultancy Group and the Academy of Executive Coaching, we have worked with this simulation and experimented with introducing coaching live into the twelve-minute days. For this to be effective, the coaching cannot be longer than three minutes, as that is a quarter of the day! Through experimentation we reduced the coaching process to its minimum to help an individual process their reactivity and decide how to get into effective empathic relationship with another person, or another part of the system. I discovered we could reduce coaching to its bare essentials, and have an effective impact within three minutes by using the following core questions and interventions:

- What do you need from these three minutes?
- Who do you need to relate to?
- What are you feeling right now? Go into your body and check out what feelings you are experiencing.
- What do you think the other person or people are feeling and needing?
- How can you connect what you need with what they need?
- So what are you going to do?

This was the most minimal coaching I found we could do and still be effective. It still follows the CLEAR model of coaching: contracting, listening, exploring, actioning and reviewing, and encourages engagement at all four levels: data, behaviour, feelings, and assumptions (Hawkins and Smith, 2006). It also focuses on actual phenomena and it is important to give no space for Door A stories, but to encourage empathic connection with the other members and parts of the system.

In the 1980s, I worked supporting a culture change at the British Aerospace Airbus division. The organization was engaged in moving from a culture where problems travelled up from the hanger floor through six levels of management and solutions travelled back down through these multiple management tiers, to one where challenges were articulated from the leaders at the top and solutions were encouraged to come back up the system. This required senior leaders to break habituated patterns and, when they were stopped in the corridor by one of their staff saying they had a problem, they were encouraged not to try and solve the problem for that staff member, but instead to use one of the following responses:

- Who can best help you with that issue?
- What form of thinking support do you need to work through that situation?
- How specifically might I help you most effectively, in the five minutes I have got?

It took much effort and support to change the ingrained habits of the leaders who had been promoted because they were good at solving problems, not coaching people. However, this was essential to fundamentally change the patterns in the culture, for employees to stop delegating their problems up the organization and be supported in resolving them themselves.

Team coaching

One of the most important shifts necessary for a team leader is to realize the difference between managing their team and leading it. When a team leader manages the team, they try and supervise all the individual team members and hold on to the responsibility for connecting and integrating the separate contributions. This causes team meetings to be a series of 'individuals reporting in to the boss'. When they become a team leader, they are more like the orchestrator of the collective team activities, encouraging the team to work together to address key challenges and issues and to be mutually accountable for the collective goals, not just their individual objectives. This transition requires them to be able to coach the team and not just coach the individual team members.

While individual coaching has been growing exponentially over the last thirty years, team coaching has been much slower and more recent in its development. For many years there have been team building and team development activities within the field of organizational development. These have tended to concentrate on the early stages in the life of a team and on the internal team dynamics, including how the individual team members relate to each other. Only recently has a distinctive approach to team coaching been developed (Clutterbuck, 2007, 2010; Hawkins, 2011a) that integrates four different strands: research on high-performing teams; team development approaches from organizational development; approaches from the field of coaching; and learning from the field of team sport psychology (Hawkins, 2011a, Chapter 4).

Organizations often discover that, despite having leadership teams of highly developed individuals, the team still performs at less than the sum of its parts. Much research has been carried out on the differences between a work group, a team, a good team, and a high-performing team (Katzenbach and Smith, 1993a; Hackman and Wageman, 2005; Wageman et al., 2008). Indeed, Wageman and her team showed in their research on 120 leadership teams that coaching was a key aspect of high-performing teams. Much of this coaching was provided by the team leader but also, at times, involved bringing in an external team coach. In a coaching culture, all team leaders will see coaching as a key aspect of their role, not only the coaching of individuals who are their direct reports, but also coaching the collective team to perform at more than the sum of its parts.

For team coaching to be effective and worthwhile, three enabling conditions first need to be in place: a collective endeavour, an aspiration, and a desire for help. The collective endeavour involves the team having a purpose and objectives that require them to work together and cannot be achieved by them simply working in parallel. The aspiration means that the team aspire to perform their collective endeavour at a higher level than they are doing currently. The desire for help is a recognition by the team that they need help on the journey to achieving their collective endeavour and aspiration.

In *Leadership Team Coaching* (Hawkins, 2011a), I argue that it is important for team coaching to focus on the team performance as well as the team dynamic and to focus on how the team engages externally with all its key stakeholders as well as internally with each other. In addition, the team needs to focus on its collective learning and enabling the learning and development of all its members. I define this form of systemic team coaching in this way:

> *Systemic team coaching* is a process by which a team coach works with a whole team, both when they are together and when they are apart. In this way they are helped to improve their collective performance, how they work together and how they develop their collective leadership in order to more effectively engage with all their key stakeholder groups to jointly transform the wider business.

I distinguish this from team development, which I define as:

> any process carried out by a team, with or without assistance from outside, to develop its capability and capacity, to work well together.

And from team building:

> any process used to help a team in the early stages of team development.

Team facilitation:

> a process where a specific person (or persons) is asked to facilitate the team by managing the process for them so they are freed up to focus on the task.

And team process consultancy:

> a form of team facilitation where the team consultant sits alongside it while it carries out its meetings or planning sessions and provides reflection and review on 'how' the team is going about its task.

In *Leadership Team Coaching* (Hawkins, 2011a), I developed a model of the five disciplines of high-performing teams:

1. *Commissioning*. For a team to be successful, it needs a clear commission from those who bring it into being. This includes a clear purpose and defined success criteria by which the performance of the team will be assessed. Once there is a clear commission, the role of the board (in the case of a leadership team) or more senior management (in the case of other teams) is to appoint the right team leader that they believe can deliver this mission. The team leader then

has to select the right team members who will have the right chemistry and diversity to work well together so that the team performs at more than the sum of its parts. Jim Collins (2001) describes this process as 'getting the right people on the bus'.

2. *Clarifying*. Having ascertained its commission from outside itself and assembled the team, one of the first tasks is for the new team to internally clarify and develop its own mission. The process of creating this mission together leads to higher levels of ownership and clarity for the whole team. This mission includes the team's:

- purpose
- strategic goals and objectives
- core values
- compelling vision for success
- collective key performance indicators
- protocols and ways of working
- roles and expectations.

3. *Co-creating*. Having a clear purpose, strategy, process, and vision that everyone has signed up to is one thing, living it is a completely different challenge. If the mission is not going to remain a well-constructed group of words, but have a beneficial and impactful influence on performance, the team needs to constantly attend to how they work together both creatively and generatively. This involves the team noting when it is functioning well at more than the sum of its parts, as well as noting and changing its own negative patterns, self-limiting beliefs, and assumptions.

4. *Connecting*. Being well commissioned, clear about what you are doing, and co-creative in how you work together is necessary but not sufficient. The team only makes a difference if the members collectively and individually connect and engage with all their critical stakeholders. It is through how the team engages in new ways to transform the stakeholder relationships that the team drives improvement in their own and the organization's performance.

5. *Core learning*. This fifth discipline sits in the middle and above the other four, and is the place where the team stand back, reflect on their own performance and multiple processes, and consolidate their learning ready for the next cycle of engagement. This discipline is also concerned with supporting and developing the performance and learning of every team member. Collective team learning and all the individual team members' learning go hand in hand and all high-performing teams are committed to both processes.

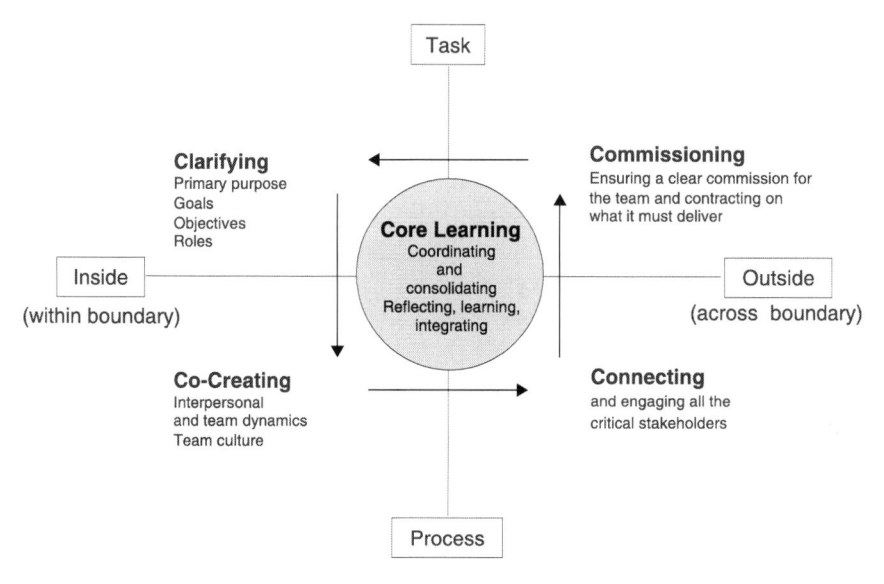

Figure 7.1 The five disciplines of high-performing teams.

Task

Clarifying
Primary purpose
Goals
Objectives
Roles

Commissioning
Ensuring a clear commission for the team and contracting on what it must deliver

Core Learning
Coordinating and consolidating
Reflecting, learning, integrating

Inside
(within boundary)

Outside
(across boundary)

Co-Creating
Interpersonal and team dynamics
Team culture

Connecting
and engaging all the critical stakeholders

Process

The high-performing leadership team needs to be effective in all five of these disciplines. Although there is an implied progression for moving through these disciplines, this will change depending on the context, stage of development, and needs of the group. Also, the process is iterative and the five disciplines create a continuous cycle. As the context in which the team works changes, the team and in particular its leader has to engage in *re-commissioning* with those that provide its legitimacy to operate. Politicians have to seek a new mandate from their electorate; leadership teams have to achieve new backing from their board and shareholders for their next transformational change, and so on. This then requires *re-clarification* of the internal mission as a team and *co-recreating* new ways of working effectively together to deliver the new agenda, while *re-connecting* with their stakeholders who need to be aligned and brought into the change.

To effectively coach a team requires the capability and methodology to work with each of these five disciplines and to connect them. Although there have been many thousands of skilled individual coaches over the last thirty years, we are only just beginning to develop skilled systemic team coaches. However, team leaders are beginning to recognize that in addition to coaching and developing each of their team members, another of their key roles is to coach the collective team in how it performs and engages both internally in its team dynamics and externally with its stakeholders.

One of the first tasks for team leaders in coaching their collective team is to address Discipline 3 of how the team co-creates and to look at how to improve the productivity of team meetings. This process can be helped by introducing a coaching style to help the meeting process. Team coaching, at its best, not only develops high-performing teams, but assists the organization in creating more effective working between teams, as shown in the following case study.

Case study: Yeovil District Hospital Foundation Trust
The Hospital had undertaken a review of its organizational structure and decided that it needed three important changes:

- move from ten directorates to three divisions;
- introduce medical leadership into each of the three divisions;
- delegate more operational management to the three divisions so the executive could focus more on the external and future strategic work of the hospital.

However, they recognized that they needed to use these structural changes to also enable a cultural change and avoid replacing ten silos with three large silos. The executive team hired a team coach and from their joint inquiries became clear that the coaching needed to focus not just on the executive team (1), the three new divisional teams (2, 3, 4), and the board (5), but on the connections between them (a, b, c). The need to shift these relationships also needed to be addressed in the context of what needed to shift in the culture of the relationships

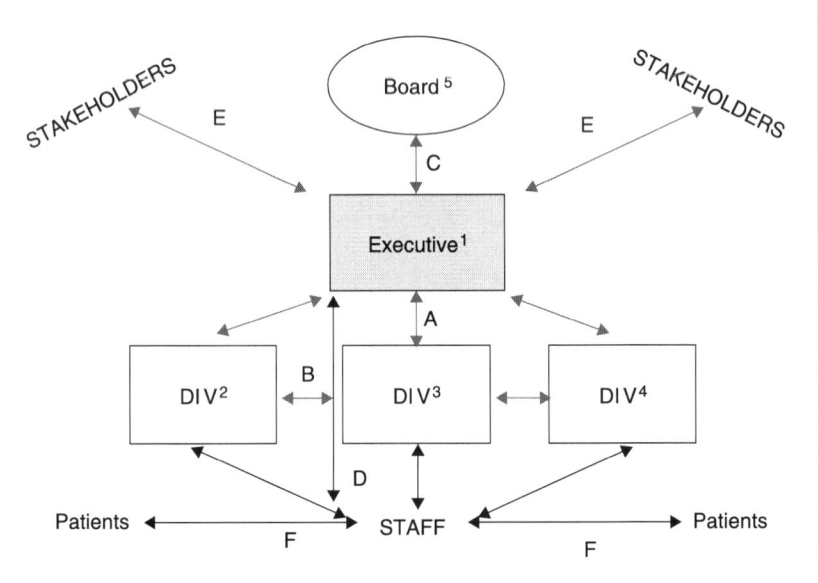

Figure 7.2 The Foundation Trust; five key teams, six critical relationships.

between management and front-line staff (d), and front-line staff and patients (f), as well as between the executive and board and the external stakeholders, such as commissioning, regulatory, and funding bodies (e).

The coaching included sessions for the five key teams (including the board) as well as sessions where the different teams worked together, clarifying to each other their own roles and goals and what they needed from the other teams to most effectively achieve their objectives and the overall success of the hospital.

The coaching style team meeting

For many years, I and my colleagues had been using the CLEAR coaching model – Contract, Listen, Explore, Action, Review – as a way of structuring coaching, counselling, and supervision processes, before one of the leaders on a leadership development programme said to us: 'I could use this to run my meetings and the workshop sessions of my project group'. Since that helpful creative leap, I have used the model as part of coaching executive teams and for facilitating project and change team workshops.

- *Contracting*: 'What is it we need to achieve today? What would success from today look like? How do we need to work together to achieve that?'
- *Listening*: 'Let us get all the different perspectives, hopes, and fears out on the table, and make sure they are all heard before we explore ways forward'.
- *Explore*: 'Let us brainstorm all the elements that might be needed to move forward. What can we experiment with today?'
- *Action*: 'So what are we committed to doing? Who will do what, by when? What support is necessary? How can we start living that in our meeting today?'
- *Review*: 'So what worked well in this session? What could we do even better next time we work like this?'

A number of leadership teams and boards have used this model to restructure their regular meetings.

1. Start with a *check-in* and *contract* for the outcomes.
2. *Listen* to the updates and new challenges.
3. *Explore issues in greater detail* to ensure generative team dialogue that produces genuinely new thinking on a critical area of performance.
4. *Agree the action* to be taken and demonstrate embodied and energetic commitment to making it happen.

5. Finish with a check-out or *review*. This can involve sharing appreciation of what has been helpful in the meeting, or individuals' commitments about what they will be taking away and doing differently.

The coaching style engagement events

The team leader, once they have learnt to coach their team on its internal functioning, can look at Discipline 4 of 'connecting with stakeholders' and discover how to bring a coaching approach to these important encounters.

> Many years ago I was working with a large international financial company helping to facilitate a company-wide culture change. Early in the assignment I was invited to their annual leadership conference. At great expense, the 120 most senior members in the company, who had flown in from many parts of the world, spent their days in serried rows, being lectured by each member of the executive team. Most were waiting for the late afternoon golf challenge or the late night drinking, where the important networking happened. I asked the executives, who were all experts in investment proposals, what their return on investment was from this very expensive annual conference. It was a question they had never considered and were unable to answer. However, it provided enough disquiet to open up an interest in how the following year's conference could create more value for the organization.
>
> The following year's conference was a major break with tradition. The planning started by contracting with the senior team how they believed their senior leaders and managers needed to be different by the end of the conference. I asked them to draw up a list of what they would like, by the end of the conference, their staff to be:
>
> - thinking differently
> - feeling differently
> - saying differently
> - doing differently.
>
> From this starting point it was possible to design an event, working jointly with a carefully chosen band of internal facilitators drawn from every level and function of the organization. This design was based on asking: 'What would create the difference articulated in the outcome goals?' Instead of serried ranks, there were round tables, each with a coach or facilitator. Instead of the 'tell and sell' from each executive on the stage, the executive members spoke about the challenges that the company had to address, and then posed a number of challenging

questions they wanted the table groups to grapple with. The table coach had been trained and briefed in how to maximize whole-group involvement, creative and divergent thinking, synthesizing and connecting different ideas that emerged, and encouraging the group to engage in collective and innovative feedback. The interesting and creative dialogues moved out of the late night drinking in the bars and on to the conference floor, where everyone was engaged in co-creating the collective way forward for the organization.

Harvesting the learning

In the opening chapter, I told the story of asking chief executives and HR directors who employ a lot of external coaches:

> How many coaching conversations do you think happen every month in your organization?

Very few had a clear idea but most estimated that it was in the thousands, particularly if you include coaching conversations by line managers and not just formal external and internal coaching. Then follows a simple but challenging question:

> How does your organization learn from these thousands of coaching conversations?

They are usually puzzled but curious about how coaching can lead to organizational learning and demonstrable organizational benefit.

In large organizations, there may be many coaching relationships that occur in parallel. Three- and four-way contracting and evaluation processes (see Chapters 4 and 5) will help the learning to move beyond the confines of the coaching room but this learning can be restricted to the few people who have been involved in the contracting and 360-degree feedback processes. However, there will be a great deal of organizational learning that, due to the confidentiality of most coaching contracts, remains unrealized. Bath Consultancy Group developed a methodology for preserving the appropriate confidentiality of the one-to-one coaching relationship, while at the same time helping the organization learn from the myriad of coaching relationships it was sponsoring and from the collective insights of the external and internal coaching pools. This approach, termed 'Harvesting the Learning', has four stages:

1. Bringing together, at regular intervals, the community of internal and external coaches to hear the challenges the organization is

experiencing, providing a forum for questions about the organization's strategy, and its plan for the development of its business, its organization, culture, leaders, and people.
2. Then working with all the coaches in supervision trios (coach, supervisor, and observer) on key coaching relationships with managed confidentiality. The observer is given a pro-forma to capture some of the emerging themes, including:
   (i) Clarity and alignment concerning the direction of the organization and what this direction requires from leaders and managers.
   (ii) The organizational culture, including the five levels of artefacts, patterns of behaviour, mindsets, emotions, and motivational roots (see Chapter 3).
   (iii) Connections and disconnections across the organization.
   (iv) Connections and disconnections with stakeholders.
   (v) How coaching is perceived.

   Each person has thirty minutes in each role, and there is some time for feedback to the supervisor on their supervision – thus providing additional developmental learning.
3. The groups of three are then asked to look for patterns emerging across the themes collected from all three supervision sessions. We will have sometimes provided a short input and handout on systemic pattern identification. These patterns will be entered on to Post-its® and posted on different themed flip chart boards. The groups then split up into small groups by each themed board and work on clustering the emerging themes, identifying the patterns that connect them, and then feeding these back into the whole group. They are asked to identify the key patterns that will enable or block the organization in meeting its strategic and developmental objectives.
4. These enabling and blocking patterns are then brought together and a dialogue is facilitated between senior executives and the coaches on these emerging key themes. This can either be at the same event or at a later meeting between the senior leadership team and a representative group of internal and external coaches. Having explored the emerging themes, the dialogue can focus on how coaching can contribute more effectively to the next stages of the organization's development.

This process requires facilitation from a consultant that is not only an experienced coach and skilled coaching supervisor, but also someone who understands organizational strategy, culture change, systemic dynamics, and organizational development. Most importantly, this facilitator needs to translate between the strategic and business language of senior executives and the more process language of the coaches. There is a shortage of people who can connect the different domains of organizational life: the strategic and commercial, the organizational development, and personal perceptions, motivations, and development.

This full process for harvesting the learning may sound rather daunting for many coaching communities in the early stages of their development, but simpler forms of the process can be adopted as part of the annual review of the coaching community. A case study of such an annual review is included below.

> **Case study: Electricity Supply Board**
> The Electricity Supply Board (ESB), Ireland's premier electricity utility company, used its recent coaching conference to address the challenge: 'How can we collectively double the value of coaching in our company?' By stating the conference theme this way, they were setting a frame that sought to connect the work of the coaching community to how the organization created value.
>
> At the conference they facilitated an active inquiry process and clustered the emerging themes. The following are highlights of themes that emerged and were clustered by the different sub-groups. These focus mainly on the way coaching operates, but some of the later themes move on to areas of developing a coaching culture in the wider organization:
>
> *Utilization of coaches*
> - ensure all coaches are coaching;
> - 'core' coaches – fully occupied;
> - important that coaches retain their skill – we have a lot of 'not very' confident coaches – need to maintain the skill.
>
> *Development of coaches*
> - coaching should be seen as development opportunity for the coach – not as an additional task;
> - coaches should ensure their own continuing professional development (CPD);
> - supervision, triads, and 'lunch and learn sessions';
> - conference part of CPD and a 'recovery' day for coaches;
> - external speakers valuable support to coaches;
> - coaching coordinators are proactively interacting with coaches – are seen as the first point of contact and support for their coaches;
> - examine the wider role of coaching in the ESB where the assignment isn't work- or performance-related (e.g. career or lifestyle).
>
> *Coaching process*
> - raise profile of coaching in the businesses – examine PR etc., and link with performance processes;
> - preparation and learning critical to success of coaching assignment;

- more in-depth matching of coaches and clients;
- formal coaching needs to be integrated into HR processes;
- greater buy-in to the value of the formal coaching process;
- further embed the first 100 days initiative – coaching should be seen as positive and not remedial.

Communications
- greater evaluation of the value of coaching and alignment to business and corporate strategy;
- constant communication required between coaching coordinators and line managers to ensure value of coaching is understood;
- coaches should be ambassadors for coaching.

Coaching offering
- make coaching available at all levels – especially where major change a factor – plan interventions early – don't wait on the flood;
- make available earlier in career, e.g. on completion of apprenticeship/study, etc.;
- explore 'group' coaching as opportunity for development.

Supervision
- coaches leading their own learning – will enhance the quality of coaching;
- wealth of learning from group/team supervision;
- develop coaching supervision structure.

Performance management
- line managers not abdicating responsibility to coach;
- managers should ensure clear targets and that measurement takes place;
- key performance indicators for managers to ensure coaching/development is happening for staff – survey to measure effectiveness.

Coaching style for managers
- training for line managers to develop their coaching skills;
- line managers should adopt a coaching style;
- line managers should give better feedback – accomplishments, performance, quality conversations;
- coaching style not just a 'nice manager' skill but a necessary skill to deliver improved performance;
- examine competencies as a way of developing a coaching style for managers and adopt through performance management.

These areas helped the ESB to formulate the next stage in their coaching strategy, which involved five project teams drawn from the coaching community working on key emerging areas of development:

1. Embedding a first 100 days coaching approach for people in new roles that has gradually developed since 2008.
2. Team coaching offered for developing leadership teams and project teams.
3. Coaching and developing others to become a core leadership skill for all senior managers, and provide development of this.
4. Focusing on a reduced number of internal coaches, but ensuring these are fully utilized and continuously developed.
5. Developing supervision for all internal coaches and a number of internal supervisors.

Conclusion

So in this fourth step on the journey to becoming a coaching culture, coaching moves beyond the confidential formal coaching sessions for the privileged few, and starts to happen informally in corridor coaching sessions and in team meetings and engagement events. For many organizations, this is a fundamental shift in their organizational culture and will not be achieved in short measure. It can only be sustained if the next two steps of the journey are also put in place: (i) build the coaching culture into the HR processes of the organization (Step 5, Chapter 8), and (ii) train and support managers in developing coaching skills (Step 6, Chapter 9).

8 Step 5: Coaching becomes embedded in the HR and performance management processes of the organization

Introduction

There are two common sayings that are relevant for establishing a sustainable coaching culture:

> What gets measured is what gets done.

> What gets measured is what is easy to measure.

Many organizations fall into the trap of extolling the importance of coaching and their commitment to constantly developing their people, but fail to build in ways that set objectives and measure them. Often this is because it is easier to measure the financial and task delivery objectives than the people development objectives. The organization that wants to create a coaching culture should not let this deter it from ensuring that coaching is part of all aspects of its HR strategy, operations, and measurement.

In Chapter 3, I showed how the coaching culture needs to be linked to all the main HR strategies, which, in turn, need to be linked to the business strategies. These strategic links provide the grounding for coaching and a coaching style to become part of all the HR processes as well as how the HR department conducts its business. This is illustrated by the work of the UK Department of Work and Pensions.

> ***Case study: UK Department of Work and Pensions***
> In response to its 2008 Capability Review, the UK Department of Work and Pensions launched four important linked HR strategies: a 'People Strategy', 'Skills Strategy', 'Leadership and Management Development Strategy', and 'People Performance'. They then reviewed all their coaching activities to ensure they

aligned to effectively deliver these HR strategies. Their coaching strategy was linked to delivering strategic priorities:

- *Learning and continuous improvement* – coaching helps everyone in DWP learn and continuously improve;
- *Professional capability* – coaching supports those who are working towards accreditation/qualifications and mentoring supports professional career development;
- *Performance improvement* – a coaching style is used by line managers as part of our 'People Performance' process to improve performance and personal development planning;
- *Leadership and management capability* – coaching and mentoring is a key tool in building leadership and management capability;
- *Customer service* – coaching is used to deliver a more customer focused efficient service by embedding technical related training and encouraging our people to engage in coaching conversations where appropriate with our customers;
- *Change capability* – coaching is available to senior teams and individuals engaged in business transformation;
- *Employee engagement* – a strong coaching and mentoring culture will increase employee engagement and empowerment.

In this chapter, I start by looking at how to select leaders and managers that are both coachable and able to coach. Next, I explore how to build personalized objectives and performance measures for one of the most important aspects of every leader and manager's role – that is, how they coach and develop the people that report to them. Then, I look at how this can be linked to reward.

Selecting those who can coach and are coachable

In their research on top leadership teams, Wageman et al. (2008: 97) showed that so-called 'dangerous derailers' can undermine the establishment of high-performing teams. Dangerous derailers are team members who: 'refuse to play the game'; 'may not commit to the team norms'; 'refuse to accept the chief executive's leadership'; and 'may not agree with the enterprise's strategy, its operating model or the team's main purposes'.

> The trouble with derailers: they tend to bring everyone down with them. Worse they tend to be closed to corrective feedback and relatively immune to coaching.
>
> (Wageman et al., 2008: 99)

They warn:

> Beware of any team member who does the following:
>
> - Frequently complains about and criticizes others in public
> - Brings out the worse in other members
> - Attacks people instead of criticizing the issues
> - Talks in the hall but not in the room
> - Constantly disagrees with everyone and everything
> - Displays chronic discrepancies between public word and private actions
> - Claims to understand her behaviour but seems unable to change.
>
> (Wageman et al., 2008: 101)

In his leadership of the cultural change process at the BBC, Greg Dyke distinguished between 'cynics', who were similar to Wageman's 'derailers', and who on principle would undermine any change process and oppose all leadership from others, and 'sceptics', who would constructively challenge change proposals but were open to being convinced (Dyke, 2004). Dyke introduced a change process called 'eliminate the cynics', which included removing any senior employee that provided negative copy about the BBC for the external media, rather than address their criticisms internally. This was balanced by massive encouragement for all staff to actively challenge their bosses on anything they thought was hindering progress or blocking creativity.

It can be costly to sack derailers, in terms of time, compensation, and possible litigation. The best approach is to avoid hiring them in the first place. The most effective way of spotting a potential derailer in the selection process is to ask all interviewees to describe the biggest failure in their last role and what was its cause. The potential derailer will immediately demonstrate their capacity for blaming others and how they were the victim of circumstances. The non-derailer will show in their narrative how they were part of the problem, what they did wrong, and what they have learnt from it.

Other managers who are difficult to coach and develop include those who have strong narcissistic personality structures (Kets de Vries, 2006), show addictive behaviours or denial patterns, or who tend to bully staff. One HR leader I interviewed explained how they recruited for values, rather than skills, on the grounds that with the right values, you can develop the skills, but without alignment to the company values, the skills will not help the company move forward.

The selection process should also ascertain the coaching capability of the prospective manager or leader. Two selection processes are helpful here:

(i) arrange for a live coaching session with a current manager of the level the applicant would have to manage and lead; and

(ii) present the applicant, either verbally or in written form, a series of people scenarios and staff dilemmas that may be brought to them, and ask them how they would address them.

A combination of the two can be used where the interviewer explains that they are going to role-play someone who the applicant would be responsible for leading, managing, and developing. In the role-play, the interviewer introduces some typical problems, dilemmas, and requests. Some organizations have used actors to enact these typical scenarios.

Coaching can also make a contribution to shifting the demographic mix of leaders and managers in an organization. Many organizations have to combat institutional sexism or racism to achieve a better representation of women at senior levels or a better mix of people from different racial or national backgrounds. Coaching can be a critical component of white awareness or gender awareness programmes (Ryde, 2009), and management training can be geared to help shift the gender balance (see the case study on the European Commission in Chapter 6). The cross-company mentoring programme designed to help more women progress to board positions, illustrated in Chapter 5, shows how coaching and mentoring can shift culturally embedded mindsets in both parties.

Managing non-performance

I often ask those attending leadership development programmes how much time they spend managing their staff's non-management or mismanagement of issues and tasks they should be responsible for. They typically state from five to eighty per cent, which represents a large proportion of their time. Most managers have been successful in their careers because they are good at solving problems, so their first response to being presented with a problem by their subordinates is to solve the problem for them. This inevitably makes their subordinates less capable and dependent and themselves overworked and frenetic.

Good managers realize that they are responsible not only for getting the work done on time, at the right quality, and within budget, but also for developing the capacity of their staff. This often leads them to improve their own skills in coaching and developing their staff, including providing them with support to increase their own capacity to solve their own problems.

The difficulty comes when staff members solve their own problem in ways that the manager thinks are 'wrong' and will fail to deliver the result required. At this point, many managers revert from coach role to being directive and telling the staff member what to do. This can produce a pendulum effect whereby the staff member is unclear whether they are trusted and empowered or not and can feel undermined.

A third approach is needed that I call 'holding the challenge in the room', supportively holding the person to the challenges that need to be addressed. In this approach, the manager follows the following four steps:

1. *Facilitative coaching.* When the staff member brings the problem, the first response is to ask them catalytic questions, such as:
   (a) 'How could you handle this issue?'
   (b) 'What are the options?'
   (c) 'What are the pros and cons and consequences of each option?'
   This might lead the staff member to arrive at their own adequate solution quite quickly.
2. *Confronting the gap.* However, if the staff member is not capable of doing so or arrives at an answer the manager judges to be inadequate, the manager can avoid reverting to telling them what to do, by directly naming their concerns about the gap between their solution and the goal that needs to be achieved. Examples of how this might be voiced are:
   (a) 'I cannot see how your solution is going to meet the requirements of our customer X (or other stakeholder).'
   (b) 'If you do it that way, how will you ensure that it happens on time and within budget?'
   (c) 'How will your solution manage to connect with the other projects that are going on?'
3. *Challenge by naming the concern.* If the staff member still does not arrive at a solution that is satisfactory to the manager, the job of the manager is to make clear their own dissatisfaction live in the room. Examples of how this might be voiced are:
   (a) 'I am still not confident that this will meet the requirements of X.'
   (b) 'I am sitting here not convinced this will happen on time or within budget.'
   (c) 'What are we going to do to meet my needs for reassurance that this is going to deliver what is necessary?'
4. *Conclude* by agreeing what will meet the role requirements and concerns of both of you and decide *what* will happen by *when*, by *whom*, and *how* it will be reviewed. It also needs to be agreed at this stage what the consequences will be if the action is not taken. When the under-performance is serious, this may include verbal and written formal warnings.

Coaching as part of the balance scorecard

In setting personal objectives, many organizations use some form of the balanced scorecard approach. The balanced scorecard was first developed in the 1990s (Kaplan and Norton, 1992, 1996) as a way of translating organizational vision and mission into measurable and personalized objectives. The original four perspectives were:

- *Financial* – a few relevant high-level financial measures (reflecting the shareholder perspective).
- *Customer* – how can we add more value to our customers?
- *Internal business processes* – how can we become more efficient and effective?
- *Learning and growth* – how can we continue to improve and create greater value for all our stakeholders?

Since its early development, the balanced scorecard approach has been used to help create both individual objectives and key performance indicators that are aligned to the mission and strategy of the organization. Whatever their specific task role, all leaders and managers should have in their objectives, or balanced scorecard, both task outputs and outcome objectives that can be measured, as well as clear objectives for how they will add value through developing the capacities and capabilities of people they lead and manage. This requires exploring with every leader and manager in their performance setting meetings the following questions:

- How do their team of direct reports need to raise their performance in the coming year (team balanced scorecard)?
- To achieve that performance improvement, what do their direct reports individually and collectively need to learn and develop in the coming year?
- How will they as the leader coach and enable this learning and development to achieve the performance change?
- How will they coach their team to perform and function at more than the sum of its parts?
- How do they need to develop their coaching and developing skills and style to better achieve the individual and collective learning and development of their team of direct reports?

This ensures that the leader is being performance managed on their ability to add value through those they lead, and not just on their own task delivery. Also, that the leader is constantly attending to improving their own capacity to develop and coach others.

This exploration then needs to be translated into the balanced scorecard and key performance measures for that person.

The development conversation

Many organizations choose to separate the formal performance review conversations from conversations that focus on the development of the individual employee. Some do this by having these at separate times of the year, but with the same person (usually the manager to whom they report directly). Traditionally, development conversations were tacked on to the end of year appraisals and focused on what training courses the individual might be sent on. In the last thirty years, there has been a great deal of research and innovation in adult learning at work and much has been written about the learning organization. This work has pointed the way to a much richer variety of learning opportunities and a recognition that learning is far more effective when:

- it focuses on real issues;
- the learner is hungry to learn;
- the learner has the opportunity to combine theoretical and experiential learning, cognitive and emotional ways of engaging; and
- the learner can put their learning into practice with others as soon as possible.

When focusing on short-term development, useful questions include:

- What have you learnt and developed this year that you did not know how to do last year?
- What do you need to learn and develop this coming year?
- How can you best learn and develop those capabilities
- Who has skills that you could learn from?
- What coaching and mentoring might support your learning?

Other organizations like the development conversation to take place with a different senior manager. When we worked for the large private equity company, 3i, they ensured that all staff had a formal development conversation with their 'boss's boss' every two years. This enabled the focus to move away from short-term performance and onto long-term development of the individual and how they could maximize their potential within the organization. As well as being of benefit to the individual, these conversations had a key role in retaining good staff and alerting senior leadership to talent that needed to be developed and fast-tracked. One of the most common reasons that talented staff give for leaving is because they do not think their potential is recognized, or that they are developing as fast as they might elsewhere.

Questions that can be usefully built in to this development conversation include:

- 'What would you like to be doing in five years' time?' – ascertaining the personal ambition;
- 'What capacities, capabilities and competencies do you need to develop to achieve that ambition?' – jointly ascertaining the development needed;
- 'How might we design learning opportunities, formal and informal, on and off the job that might help you acquire and develop these?' – jointly planning a learning journey;
- 'What formal or informal coaching and mentoring might help support and accelerate this development?' – jointly planning coaching and mentoring support;
- 'What under-utilized talents do you think you have that the organization could make better use of?' – spotting hidden or under-utilized talents;
- 'How might you use your experience and skills to develop the learning of others, through coaching, mentoring, facilitating or providing training inputs?' – exploring under-utilized development resources in the individual.

One of the most under-utilized modes of learning is teaching, and often you do not fully learn something until you have taught it to others.

It is important to remember that all development conversations should be conducted in a coaching style (see Chapter 7) and that managers and leaders often need training in how to do this effectively. A good place to start this development is to build feedback into every development conversation and performance review. This can be done by the individual providing feedback to the reviewer at the end of the meeting: 'What has been most helpful in the way you have conducted this review has been . . .'; 'Future reviews would be even more helpful if you also . . .'.

Linking to reward

It is important not to move too quickly in building reward measures linked to the coaching aspects of a person's job, as this can quickly lead to managers seeing coaching as another task they have to 'tick the box' of having done to guarantee their bonus. It is important that the coaching and development objectives are allowed to be developed and trialled for the first few years, unencumbered by a link to reward. In time, it may be possible and advisable to move to a reward system that balances four aspects:

- the overall performance of the business;
- the performance of the leader's own division or team;

- their personal performance; and
- how they have enabled the improved performance of others.

This ensures that the leader is being rewarded for what they enable others to achieve with less focus on their own task delivery. It is clearly the last of these four elements that most directly focuses on the coaching, mentoring, and development role of all managers and leaders and a key aspect of how they create value for the organization.

Clearly, it is harder to create key performance indicators with hard measures for this developmental aspect of the leader's work, as there are many inseparable factors that influence people's development. Those companies that have started to go down this road have used a mixture of rigorous quantitative and qualitative measures. These include:

- the number of people the leader or manager has coached and mentored and how often;
- the number of training and facilitation inputs they have carried out;
- the feedback and scores given by those who they have coached, mentored or trained;
- 360-degree feedback, including questions regarding: (a) what others have reported they have developed in the year; (b) what enabled that support; and (c) what proportion they believe was attributable to this leader.

It is important not to build a whole bureaucracy-chasing illusive objectivity in this area (see Chapter 13). The greatest impact on behaviour and culture change comes from having this element of performance recognized and measured in a way that keeps the leader and manager focused on and accountable for this important aspect of their role.

Conclusion

In Chapter 1, I talked about the danger of managers out-sourcing the difficult conversations to the HR department, who in turn outsource them to internal or external coaches. In this chapter, I have shown ways of taking a coaching approach back to the line manager so they can become better at coaching and managing performance in a way that delivers a high-performance culture. This requires the organization to include coaching and performance management in the key performance expectations and objectives of every leader and manager, and ensure this has an equal standing with other aspects of their balanced scorecard. Linking coaching to performance management also

COACHING AND HR/PERFORMANCE MANAGEMENT 113

provides a clear foundation for evaluating the effectiveness of coaching, a theme I return to in Chapter 14. In this fifth step in creating the coaching culture, the organization needs to recruit, develop, performance manage, recognize, and promote staff in ways that support the journey. In the next chapter (Step 6), I show how managers can be trained to develop coaching skills, to implement these HR policies and approaches, and to have the difficult conversations directly.

9 Step 6: Coaching becomes the predominant style for managing throughout the organization

> Line managers are crucial if coaching is to become the predominant style of managing and working together.
>
> (Anderson et al., 2009: 11)

Introduction

The culture change needs to begin and be sanctioned at the top, but that is only the beginning. An organization cannot afford to evolve and develop at the speed of those who are leading it. Many middle managers in organizations have said to me, 'the culture here will not change until the leaders at the top change first'. My challenge back to them has been: 'Why do you think those who have been promoted because they have been successful at playing yesterday's game, are going to be the first to develop the winning game of tomorrow? Culture change can be sanctioned from the top, but needs to be driven by those in the middle of the organization – the leaders of tomorrow.'

I have worked with a number of organizations that have developed their leaders of tomorrow, not by teaching them what had made them successful, but by engaging them in project teams, often with coach facilitators, in addressing the most difficult medium- and long-term challenges the company will face. Thus they have combined their leadership and organizational development so that each supports and helps drive the other. However, if an organization wants truly to develop a coaching culture, it is necessary to go beyond leadership and talent development and help all front line managers develop a coaching style in managing both people and tasks.

Manager as coach

In Hawkins and Smith (2006), we described the continuum of coaching as going from skills coaching to performance coaching, to development coaching to transformational coaching. Increasingly, the first two types of coaching are being seen as a key part of every manager's role, rather than coaching that can be outsourced to internal or external specialists. This leaves the specialist coaches to focus on the developmental and transformational coaching.

Anderson et al. (2009: 1) carried out research on the manager as coach for the Chartered Institute of Personnel and Development, in which they pointed out: 'The manager as coach is not a new idea but it has been increasingly emphasised in the last ten years (Ellinger, 2005)'. They emphasize the use of coaching skills in the role of managers and highlight research (Hutchinson and Purcell, 2007) that shows the importance of front line managers in 'translating organizational imperatives into practice', encouraging discretionary effort from their team members, and in developing their staff. Yet they point out that 'the aspiration for all managers to be able to develop the full range of skills and techniques that might be expected from an external or internal specialist coach is unrealistic and inappropriate' (p. 12).

Line managers have many different roles, competing priorities, and increasing resource and time constraints, and for some coaching will be seen as yet another demand. This can often lead to a large rift between the rhetoric of line manager as coach and the daily reality (BlessingWhite, 2008; CIPD, 2008).

Anderson and colleagues' (2009) research involved: discussions with 95 representatives from 69 organizations; a survey of 500 managers from ten different organizations; and case studies of four organizations. From all these responses they developed a model of two levels of coaching characteristics in managers, which they called 'primary coaching characteristics' and 'mature coaching characteristics'. The primary coaching characteristics are:

- a development orientation to their staff;
- a performance orientation;
- the ability to provide effective feedback;
- skills in planning and goal setting.

The mature coaching characteristics are:

- powerful questioning and inquiry skills;
- using the ideas generated by others;
- more shared decision making;
- encouraging problem solving in others.

The primary characteristics were more widely spread across all those researched and clearly are a necessary precursor to developing the more mature characteristics. Anderson et al. found no correlation between these characteristics and any particular group based on such factors as age, experience or gender. However, more mature coaching characteristics were found in more senior managers. This they believed was due to more senior managers being more confident and skilled in ways of managing people.

Like Ellinger (2005) and Anderson et al. (2009), I believe it is unrealistic that all managers can become coaches, and that for an organization to be successful in the current social and economic climate, it is important that all managers have a coaching style to the way they manage, at least at the primary level. I also believe that the journey to creating a coaching culture only matures when the organization starts to develop coaching skills across all its management population.

Key coaching skills every manager should have

We saw in Chapter 8 that developing a coaching style for managers involves first developing an approach to managing that combines a performance orientation with a responsibility for developing all staff. This requires managers: to be clear about the performance objectives for the organization and how they translate into team and individual goals for all their staff; set clear performance expectations; provide quality feedback to staff on their current performance; and help develop their staff in improving their performance. Only when these primary coaching orientations are established can managers progress to more mature coaching characteristics, when they can adopt a more participative and developmental style to the way they manage that is based on a more mature coaching approach.

However, many organizations that I looked at have been slow to recognize that this requires all managers to develop core coaching skills and that this should be built into all aspects of their management training: from induction to training courses, to the coaching and mentoring they themselves receive on the job. Being well coached by your own manager is one of the best ways to develop your own coaching ability. In looking at some of the core elements of the best companies I studied, I arrived at the following eleven key elements of a basic coaching skills curriculum for managers.

1. *What is coaching?* Begin with a clear framework that defines coaching and coaching skills. These definitions need to distinguish between different forms of coaching (e.g. skill, performance, developmental, transformational), and the marked difference between learning coaching skills as a manager and becoming a professional coach. Also, the differences between formal and

informal coaching, between individual coaching and team coaching, and between reflective coaching and live coaching on the job.

2. *Structuring coaching conversations.* It is important for managers to have simple models for structuring coaching conversations. Many organizations use the GROW model (Whitmore, 2002) or the CLEAR model (Hawkins and Smith, 2006). Others have adapted these to their own culture and environment. Parts of the Royal Navy took the CLEAR model and translated it into an easy to remember process that their managers could have on a small card they carried around with them (see Figure 9.1).

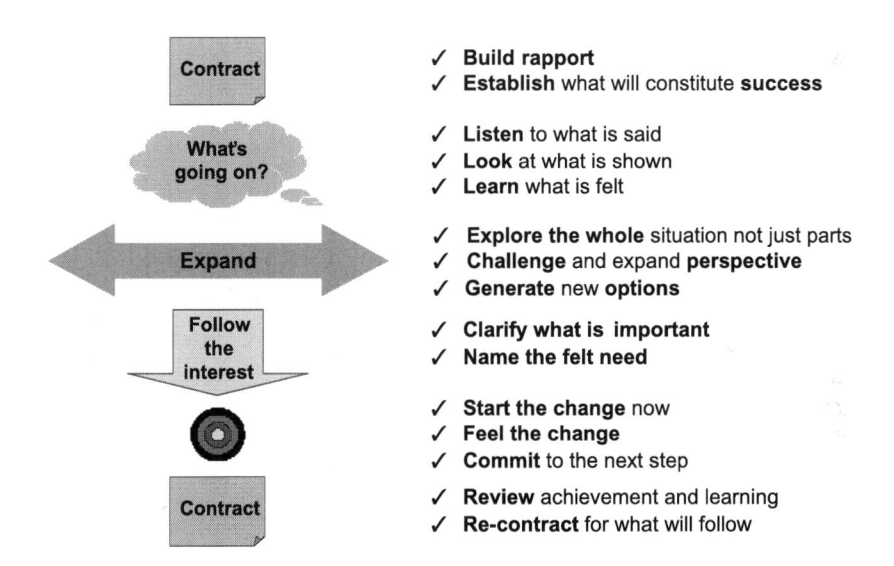

Contract
- ✓ **Build rapport**
- ✓ **Establish** what will constitute **success**

What's going on?
- ✓ **Listen** to what is said
- ✓ **Look** at what is shown
- ✓ **Learn** what is felt

Expand
- ✓ **Explore the whole** situation not just parts
- ✓ **Challenge** and expand **perspective**
- ✓ **Generate** new **options**

Follow the interest
- ✓ **Clarify what is important**
- ✓ **Name the felt need**

- ✓ **Start the change** now
- ✓ **Feel the change**
- ✓ **Commit** to the next step

Contract
- ✓ **Review** achievement and learning
- ✓ **Re-contract** for what will follow

Figure 9.1 The Royal Navy's translation of the CLEAR model.

3. *Contracting.* It is not just in formal coaching that contracting is essential. In Chapter 7, I gave the example of helping managers to break the habit of many corridor conversations, where they would be stopped by a member of staff with a problem, which they would then try and solve for them. Only by contracting before embarking on the conversation about what was needed were they able to break the dependency and their habit of solving other people's problems for them.

Simple contracting includes being clear about (a) the purpose and outcome objectives of the conversation, (b) the roles required from both parties to make it successful, (c) the time boundaries, and (d) any necessary protocols such as confidentiality.

118 CREATING A COACHING CULTURE

4. *Four levels of engagement*. Many managers are used to attending to the *facts* of what is presented and focusing on the problem 'out there'. Coaching skills training needs to help them also focus on the *behaviours* of the person who owns the issue, as well as their *feelings* and *emotions* regarding the situation and their *assumptions* and *beliefs* which are stopping them from moving forward. Together these provide the four levels of engagement model developed by my colleague Nick Smith (Hawkins and Smith, 2006) (see Figure 9.2).

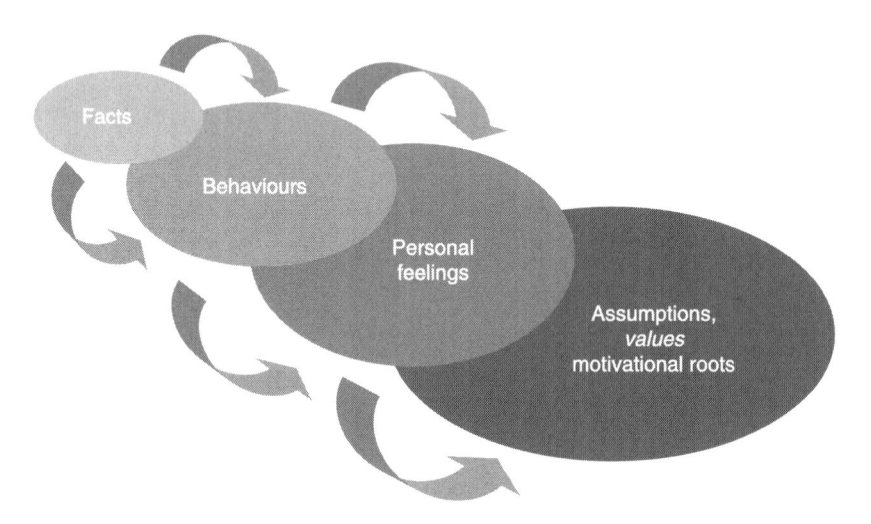

Figure 9.2 Four levels of engagement.

5. *Active listening*. Many managers who I talked to about their coaching skills training mentioned that the most powerful learning they acquired was about listening, and how listening was always something they had taken for granted without realizing how skilled a process it needed to be. In Hawkins and Smith (2006) we provide a model of four levels of listening. These four levels start by attending (Level 1), then offering accurate and active listening that involves playing back what is heard (Level 2), followed by empathic listening, where the listener resonates with the feelings of the other (Level 3), and finally pure listening, where there is space for new awareness, thinking, and being to emerge (Level 4). Real quality listening needs a great deal of practice.

6. *Torbert engagement styles*. In his excellent book on timely and transforming leadership, Bill Torbert (2004) describes how most managers over-use one style in their modes of engaging with staff – the style of *advocacy* (i.e. advocating their solution to the issue). He shows how managers can be much more effective by broadening the range of styles they use:

- *Inquiry* – using exploratory questions to open up further joint understanding of what is happening;
- *Illustrating* – using stories, images, and examples that illustrate what is possible;
- *Framing and re-framing* – offering new frames and perspectives for looking at the current situation.

7. *Powerful questioning.* The division of the Royal Navy that developed the coaching process illustrated above also provided their managers with a card with useful questions for each stage (see Figure 9.3).

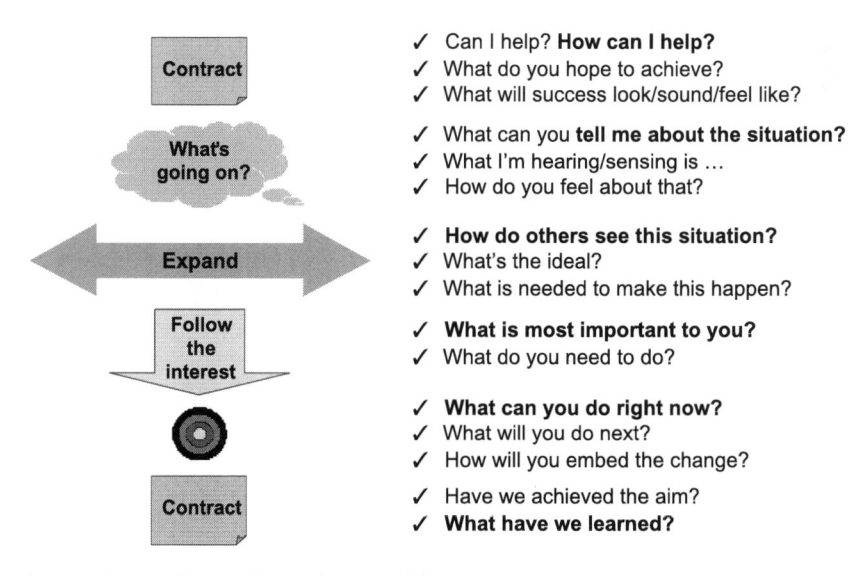

Contract
- ✓ Can I help? **How can I help?**
- ✓ What do you hope to achieve?
- ✓ What will success look/sound/feel like?

What's going on?
- ✓ What can you **tell me about the situation?**
- ✓ What I'm hearing/sensing is …
- ✓ How do you feel about that?

Expand
- ✓ **How do others see this situation?**
- ✓ What's the ideal?
- ✓ What is needed to make this happen?

Follow the interest
- ✓ **What is most important to you?**
- ✓ What do you need to do?

- ✓ **What can you do right now?**
- ✓ What will you do next?
- ✓ How will you embed the change?

Contract
- ✓ Have we achieved the aim?
- ✓ **What have we learned?**

Figure 9.3 Coaching and consulting: useful questions.

8. *Holding the challenge in the room and providing feedback.* The extent to which you can successfully challenge another person without invoking defensiveness is equal to the rapport you have first established with them, and they have experienced you as not only as someone who understands what they are talking about, but also as someone who knows what it feels like to be them. Effective challenge, like good feedback of any kind, needs to be clear, owned, regular, balanced, and specific (CORBS – see Hawkins and Shohet, 2006). It should be based on observable behaviour, not on judgements about the other's personality. Most managers are better at pointing out when an employee is not doing what is required, than they are at describing what 'good looks like' and articulating the gap that needs to be managed.

9. *Planning and goal setting.* Throughout this book I have stated how coaching that stops at the point of insight, awareness, and good intention is inadequate. This applies equally to managers using coaching skills. It is important to know how to move from exploration to specific plans for what will be done, when the action will happen, and how the employee will do it differently.

10. *Actioning.* Planning by itself is also not enough. The change needs to begin live in the meeting for it to have a good chance of being followed through later. This means inviting the employee to rehearse the opening lines of the planned conversation, showing how they will engage differently, or using other techniques that help the other move from agreement to the plan to embodied commitment.

11. *Managing progress and accountability.* The manager also needs to learn the skills of sustaining progress and ensuring the on-going accountability of their staff to what they have agreed, e.g. sending a short record of what was agreed, reviewing the progress formally in a next meeting or informally asking how the action is progressing.

Managers using a coaching style to leading their team

The above curriculum will help all managers develop the basic skills and the primary coaching characteristics. To help them move to a more mature coaching approach, they need to be helped to develop a coaching style to how they lead and manage their team. Anderson et al. (2009) show how mature coaching characteristics involve using inquiry skills that help other team members generate more collective ideas, create more shared decision making, and enable joint problem solving.

In Chapter 7, I introduced the way in which leadership teams and boards could develop a coaching approach to their meetings. Much of this is relevant to managers for improving the effectiveness of the meetings they lead. Nancy Kline (1999: 102) provides a very accessible approach to increasing the 'time to think' in meetings through creating a more participative team meeting:

At the beginning:
1. Give everyone a turn to speak.
2. Ask everyone to say what is going well in their work, or in the group's work.

Throughout:
3. Give attention without interruption during open and even fiery discussion.

4. Ask incisive questions to reveal and remove assumptions that are limiting ideas.
5. Divide into Thinking Partnerships when thinking stalls and give each person five minutes to think out loud without interruption.
6. Go around intermittently to give everyone a turn to say what they think.
7. Permit also the sharing of truth and information.
8. Permit the expression of feelings.

At the end:
9. Ask everyone what they thought went well in the meeting and what they respect in each other.

In Chapter 11, I show how a culture change project in the Swedish public sector involved new approaches to managing teams as well as coaching individuals.

Best practice in organizing coaching skills training programmes

Many organizations have introduced coaching skills programmes for their managers and team leaders. A case study in Chapter 5 refers to the programmes the BBC has introduced for line managers. In Chapter 6, I illustrated the coaching skills approach used for Partners in Ernst & Young. Here I present one of the best coaching skills programmes I came across in my research, which was the coaching programme introduced at Southern Railways.

> *Case study: The Southern Railway coaching story*
> In 2001, the South Central railway company won the franchise to run the railways in the south-east of England. They took over from the previous franchise holders, Connex, inheriting a record of poor performance, poor product, low staff morale, and a command and control directive culture. In 2003, they rebranded themselves 'Southern Railways' and invested £1 billion in new trains, stations, equipment, and depots.
> In 2004, they launched the 'Leading Southern' leadership development programme for 250 managers, which included coaching support to help the individual managers assimilate 360-degree feedback. In reviewing this leadership development process, they identified that coaching could become the major approach to linking the leadership theory training with new ways of leading and managing, which was beginning to happen back at work. So in 2005, they launched the first of their coaching programmes. In 2006, their HR strategy included the key objective:

> To develop a coaching and facilitative style of leadership.

In 2006, they launched their second coaching programme, having first to overcome some resistance from senior executives. In learning from this resistance, those leading the programme created much stronger links between coaching, leadership, and business outcomes and strategy. In 2007, they won a National Training Award for their coaching programmes and in 2008 launched their internal coaching service.

Chris Burchell, the Managing Director of Southern said in 2008:

> We are now a very successful business and delivering fantastic things to our customers. I think an element of this is definitely attributable to our focus on changing leadership style and management style. A big contributory factor to this is our coaching programme, and the learning and essence of coaching we have applied to our management training.

His statement was supported by hard business measures. These included that they had achieved the best service performance, reliability measures, and customer satisfaction scores ever achieved on this network. Staff turnover had fallen by 30 per cent and staff absence, grievances, disciplinary hearings, and tribunal figures were also all declining. Then, in 2008, the business went on to win an additional franchise, the Gatwick Express, as well as retaining the existing franchise, which runs until July 2015 without government subsidy. During this time, the business targets become more challenging, there will be significant investment (over £70m) on train and station change improvement projects and, more than ever, the capability and skills of the leadership population are critical in supporting this change.

As part of evaluation, the managers who had been involved in the programmes all had 360-degree feedback, both before and after the leadership and coaching programmes, as well as being asked to give feedback on the programme and on the changes to their own way of leading and managing and their own performance. Southern railways also decided that it was important to have external benchmarks on the quality of their coaching so the business sponsored eighty managers, including seven senior executives in achieving the Institute for Leadership and Management (ILM) Level 5 coaching qualification.

At the same time, members of the steering group were ensuring that they were monitoring the linkages to business objectives. The first linkage was to staff engagement as measured by the staff satisfaction survey. The second linkage was between this and the reduction in turnover, absences, disciplinary hearings, and grievances. The third was to service performance and reliability and the fourth to customer satisfaction. Establishing this clear chain of influence between leadership and management development and business results was essential to get the continuing support of the senior executives.

> In listening to their story, I was very impressed by the clear passion and commitment of the managing director to the journey they had been on, but even more impressed with the film they showed of front line staff talking about how things had changed, and the number of managers talking about how learning to be coaching style managers had fundamentally changed not only how they managed, but how they related to people generally. Here are just two typical quotes from managers.
>
>> For me the coaching journey has been about discovering that you can be a far more effective leader if you develop your coaching skills. Learning to be a powerful listener instead of a good talker – learning to ask the right questions makes it easier to get more from people. (Train care depot manager)
>> This isn't about coaching, it completely changes the way I think about talking to people. (Financial controller)

Supporting the coaching managers development

As with internal coaches (see Chapter 5), it is important that the training does not stop with a short workshop, but that there is further continuing development to sustain the learning and further develop the capacity of managers to coach their staff. This can be done through a variety of on-going learning methods, including:

- action learning sets
- coaching practicum groups (see Chapter 6)
- supervision groups with an experienced coach (Hawkins and Smith, 2006).

Each of these provides opportunities for six to nine managers to bring key relationships with staff they are trying to coach and develop, and actively explore how they could handle these better. Some organizations have also developed a peer coaching network and processes that encourage managers to seek support and coaching from each other across the organizations.

Conclusion

It is not possible, or appropriate, to train all managers as coaches, but all managers can be equipped with coaching skills that they can incorporate into their daily way of managing staff, running meetings or doing performance and development sessions. In some organizations, this is built into their regular management development training programmes, while in others they provide special coaching skills training and continuing support and development for the coaching work of their managers.

In Chapter 10, I explore how a coaching approach has moved beyond ways of leading and managing inside the organization to be part of how the organization's leaders and front line staff engage customers, partners, investors, regulators, and the stakeholder communities in which they operate.

10 Step 7: Coaching becomes how an organization does business with all its stakeholders

Introduction

Thus far, I have focused on creating a coaching culture within the organization, so that it permeates throughout its leadership, management, and staff, their performance management and selection. The final step is to create a coaching approach for the way that the organization does business with all its stakeholders: customers, suppliers, investors, partner organizations, regulators, and the communities in which they operate, to increase the quality and value of these relationships.

In the 1990s, the Royal Society for the Encouragement of Arts, Manufactures and Commerce (RSA, 1995) launched a very innovative inquiry process to look at 'Tomorrow's Company'. This process involved members from a wide variety of organizations across many sectors. In the report, the RSA argued that many commercial companies were too focused on delivering short-term value to their shareholders and not focusing sufficiently on delivering value to all their other stakeholders. One of the valuable outputs from their inquiry was the production of a model annual report that could be used by companies to report what they had received and what value they had generated for each of the following stakeholders:

- investors
- customers
- suppliers and partner organizations
- employees
- communities in which the company operates.

I have worked with this stakeholder model, both in companies I have chaired as well as in a number where I have been a consultant. In doing so, I have added another critical stakeholder group, albeit one that often lacks a human voice to represent it, which is the natural environment. In the past, approaches to community and social responsibility often involved companies making philanthropic donations to 'worthy causes' from their profits and publishing codes of ethical practice and values statements. To create a sustainable world, this is no longer enough. All organizations need to be accountable to all their stakeholders, human and otherwise. They need to give back more than has been received, in a long-term and sustainable way. This includes being accountable to the natural environment, 'the more than human world', so as to ensure that the organization has returned more than it has taken.

As Gregory Bateson, the great systems thinker of the twentieth century, wrote:

> In accordance with the general climate of thinking in mid nineteenth century England, Darwin proposed a theory of natural selection and evolution, in which the unit of survival was either the family line or species or sub-species or something of that sort. But today it is quite obvious that this is not the unit of survival in the real biological world. The unit of survival is organism plus environment. We are learning by bitter experience that the organism that destroys its environment destroys itself.
>
> (Bateson, 1972: 459)

As Bateson indicates, we need to recognize that both the unit of survival and the unit of high performance is never the organization. Narrowly focusing on, or competitively succeeding within, your own niche will at best lead to sub-optimization of your part of the system, and at worst to helping destroy the environment that sustains it. Success is always relational. So the organization is always in relationship to its environment, ecological niche, and systemic context.

Michael Porter, a highly influential thinker in the field of strategy, wrote with his colleague Mark Kramer, a ground breaking paper on 'shared value' for the *Harvard Business Review* (Porter and Kramer, 2011), in which they argue that part of the current economic and global crisis is due to the breakdown of alignment between company goals and social progress:

> companies . . . remain trapped in an outdated approach to value creation that has emerged over the past few decades. They continue to view value creation narrowly, optimising short-term financial performance in a bubble while missing the most important customer needs and ignoring the broader influences that determine their longer-term success.
>
> (Porter and Kramer, 2011: 63)

They go on to advocate:

> The solution lies in the principle of shared value, which involves creating economic value in a way that also creates value for society by addressing its needs and challenges. Businesses must reconnect company success with social progress . . . It is not on the margin of what companies do but at the center. We believe that it can give rise to the next major transformation of business thinking.
>
> (Porter and Kramer, 2011: 63)

Like Porter and Kramer and Bateson, I would argue that the value of any organizational change is only realized by the subsequent changes in the way it engages and creates value for all its stakeholders, not just through their product or service, but also through the quality of their relationships. Changing the internal culture of an organization is not an end in itself, but a prerequisite for creating new shared value through better coaching style relationships with customers, suppliers, partner organizations, investors, regulators, and the communities in which the organization operates.

Senior executives in all forms of organization have had to realize that they lead an enterprise that stretches from their supplier's supplier, right through to their customer's customer, and not just an organization that is bounded by the employees on their company's organizational chart.

> As organizations become more flexible, the boundaries that matter are in the minds of managers and employees . . . The traditional organizational map describes a world that no longer exists.
>
> (Hirschorn and Gilmore, 1992)

Thus to fully create a coaching culture, the executive needs to explore how a coaching culture would be helpful at all stages in the value chain and in all the key stakeholder relationships.

Coaching customers

When I was young, in the 1950s, labour was cheap, and although my family were not well off and could not afford a car, all our food and goods were delivered to us. When we did manage to buy a car, the garage would fill the car with petrol, at airports staff would check you in and issue your tickets, and at banks you had personal service. Gradually customers have learnt to do things for themselves. As we have moved into the self-service generation, staff have moved from serving to coaching the customer.

When they first introduced self-service check-ins, British Airways trained a number of their check-in staff in how to coach customers to check-in themselves. In some clothes shops, while making your own selection, you might use the services of a style coach, who will coach you on what clothes will create a distinctive wardrobe for you. In doing this, many customer coaches have learnt good basic coaching skills by:

- finding out whether the customer would like help and what the customer wants to achieve (*contracting*);
- inquiring what options the customer has already thought about or tried (*listening*);
- exploring what alternative options the customer might be interested in (*exploring*);
- supporting the customer while they try on the clothes, operate the self-service check-in, etc. (*action*);
- eliciting feedback and checking if there is additional help the customer requires (*review*).

The sales functions of many companies, be they commercial goods, manufacturing, financial or professional services, have adapted their sales training so that it has much more of a coaching approach. The most used is the SPIN selling approach, which is fundamentally a coaching approach to selling. SPIN was developed by Neil Rackham (1988) and his consulting firm, Huthwaites. They carried out extensive research, monitoring over 35,000 sales calls. SPIN stands for four key stages in the sales coaching conversation:

- Situation
- Problem
- Implication
- Need-payoff.

Rather than advocating the benefits of the product you are trying to sell, the coach-seller starts by ascertaining the customer's *situation*. Thus a lawnmower salesperson would ask the potential customer: 'What sort of lawns do you have? How big are they?' Having clarified the situation, they then proceed to inquire about the *problem*: 'What difficulties do you have with your current lawnmower? What is difficult about cutting your lawns?' Having understood the current problem, the sales coach follows up on the *implications* these problems have for the customer. Thus if the customer states that he has many trees in the middle of his lawn, which his current machine cannot cut closely around, the salesperson asks questions to ascertain what this means for the customer: untidy areas of lawn are left around each tree; it takes much longer to mow the lawn; and he has to bend over and cut these areas by hand and he has a bad back. This stage helps to build 'sales rapport' and the buyer's motivation to change. It also provides the information to help the salesperson focus on asking questions that help the customer express his explicit needs for and from a new lawnmower. The coach may then playback to the customer their understanding of what *need-payoff* the customer has: 'So, I understand you need a lawnmower that will save you from bending over, reduce the amount of time you spend each week cutting your lawns, and will cut neatly close to the trees without damaging them.'

The first salespeople that Huthwaites trained in the model showed a 17 per cent increase in their sales. Later, while working with Xerox, they discovered that in the absence of follow-up coaching for the salespeople, 87 per cent of the benefit of the training can be lost.

Many leading companies have also developed ways of involving their customers in their product development, where the customers coach the product designers and engineers in how to create a product that would best meet their needs. A classic example of this was Boeing's development of their 777 airliner, which impressively only took four years from inception to delivery, in contrast to the industry average, then about ten years. Boeing *contracted* with some of their best major airline customers (Nippon Airways, British Airways, Cathay Pacific, Delta Air Lines, Japan Airlines, Quantas, and United Airlines) to join their 'working together' group. At the first meeting in 1990, a long questionnaire was provided to each airline to ascertain the specific future needs of their passenger planes. This was then discussed with the group as it moved into a basic design specification (the *listening* phase). By January 1993, they were ready to hold a major event at their Boeing Everett factory in Washington involving designers, developers, and teams from each of their customer partners. They divided into 240 design teams of up to forty members each, which worked on individual components of the aircraft. Altogether, 1500 design issues were addressed (the *exploring* phase). Boeing then progressed this design into a full computer virtual model that could be tested, and involved customers at each phase in helping them refine and improve the design. Boeing was able to start delivering the finished plane in 1994 and it began flying commercially in 1995 (*action*). The final phase was engaging their customer group in the ways they could jointly learn from this process so that they could make future designs even better (*review*).

Using coaching skills with service users

In the public sector or civil society, a number of organizations have engaged their service users differently using a coaching approach. Those in the helping professions have arguably always used what I am now term 'coaching skills' as a key aspect of how they have engaged their clients (Hawkins and Shohet, 2006). Doctors, nurses, social workers, teachers, psychologists, and therapists have combined their professional expertise with ways of helping their clients attend to their own health, education, and well-being. Where they have failed to do so, some have argued, they disable those they are there to help (Illich, 1997). Enabling one's clients, rather than making them more dependent on one's own expertise, is even more critical in the role of development agencies helping those in the poorest and most challenged countries of the world. Oxfam developed its own coaching culture and then expanded it into their work in development projects.

> *Case study: Oxfam*
> Oxfam is one of the largest global charities working with international poverty and in its 2009–2010 annual report it illustrated how it was working with 17 million people in 64 countries. Over the last seven years, Oxfam has worked hard at developing its own coaching culture, from the senior management teams at the centre to the projects worldwide. In 2007, the coaching manager, Liz Lambert, set out their coaching strategy:
>
>> This document sets out the case for a developing coaching culture in Oxfam and outlines the broad plan to establish a coaching culture over the next three years. It is intended to give key stakeholders an understanding of the rationale and broad approach of this work.
>> Oxfam has invested in coaching for the last few years. It is recognized as an effective way of developing individual and organizational competence. Coaching is aligned with Oxfam's values:
>>
>> - *Empowerment* – through taking responsibility for their own learning, coaching can empower them to make decisions and think for themselves in order to deliver.
>> - *Accountability* – coaching supports accountability by providing a vehicle to have discussions about what we do well, and what we need to change.
>> - *Inclusivity* – coaching can challenge our perspectives and deepen our understanding of situations. It helps people to understand situations from other perspectives, enabling us to be more inclusive.
>>
>> Oxfam is concerned with social change, which takes place in environments that are complicated, unpredictable, and challenging. When working with communities, partners, and each other, putting concepts into action in these environments requires learning that is particular to that situation. A coaching approach to our interactions facilitates learning that is context specific, enabling people to deliver in the most appropriate way.
>> Coaching activities in Oxfam include:

- Internal coaches working with individuals and teams
- In-house coaching skills courses and modules
- Coaching skills developed through action learning sets on the Management and Leadership Programme
- Several senior managers working with executive coaches.

In early 2007, the Corporate Management Team decided to further support the organization to develop management capability through developing coaching as a way of working. As an organization that coaches, we can guide learning processes rather than leaving it up to chance.

Like many organizations, Oxfam had started by using external coaches and then developed internal coaches and embedded a coaching approach in their leadership development activities. Then, Liz Lambert and her colleagues wanted to take coaching to the next level, and have it as a core approach to how the front line staff worked with their partner organizations throughout their global projects.

Coaching patients

Another exciting area of coaching is that being carried out by health organizations with service users to introduce health coaching into preventative health care work for those who are likely to suffer from chronic long-term conditions in later life. Health coaching is defined as:

> A behavioural intervention that facilitates participants in establishing and attaining health-promoting goals in order to change lifestyle-related behaviours, with the intent of reducing health risks, improving self-management of chronic conditions, and increasing health-related quality of life.
>
> (Van Ryn and Heaney, 1997)

A well-evaluated use of health coaching was in Minnesota, where, in 2008, Medica launched a telephone health coaching service to 392,000 people and employed twenty-eight health coaches to do so. They estimated that 11 per cent of its members might benefit and they were contacted about the service. Of these, 20 per cent chose to enrol, nearly 4000 members. The results in the first six months for these 4000 were very impressive:

- The use of hospital inpatient resources was reduced by 18 per cent compared with similar members not enrolled.

- Emergency doctor visits fell by 12 per cent in the intervention group.
- 81 per cent had improved quality-of-life scores.
- 45 per cent showed improved cholesterol.
- 42 per cent showed a reduction in body mass index.
- 66 per cent reported an improvement in their patient activation score related to exercise.
- Members' health care expenditures dropped by US$139 per member per month after six months.

Health coaching has also been used in the UK National Health Service. In East Suffolk, Dr. Penny Newman, supported by coach/psychologist Dr. Andrew McDowell, started a project that had the following aims:

- to improve the care and lives of people with long-term conditions in East Suffolk;
- to raise awareness and responsibility in patients to improve self-care and self-management of their own long-term condition;
- to enable patients to identify their goals and develop their own personal care plans;
- to improve the consultation skills of practice nurses to include health coaching or skills in behaviour change;
- to enable the nurses to practise their skills and explore self-care with patients in longer appointments.

They trained practice nurses in coaching skills who then offered longer health coaching appointments with those at risk of long-term chronic conditions that can be affected by lifestyle and behavioural choice, such as diabetes, chronic heart disease, and stroke. The patients were required to be motivated to lifestyle change (e.g. smoking, diet, exercise) and willing to enter into a different kind of consultation (health coaching).

The project is only just getting underway in 2011, but the initial training has been well received and evaluation procedures established from the beginning.

Coaching investors

Traditionally, large public companies make large presentations to all their major investors, at least annually at the AGM, and often quarterly. Usually, board members will be on the platform at the front of the hall and the investors in serried ranks. The board present their 'tell and sell' presentations, in the hope of convincing their investors to keep investing and hopefully to invest more, thus raising the demand and the price of shares. This is then followed by a question-and-answer session and, because of the very nature of the engagement, the questions will often be critical or adversarial: shareholders trying to discover what the board have not told them; asking why the board have not done x or y; challenging the strategic directions the company is planning or their future predictions.

Some companies that I have worked with or interviewed have introduced a more coaching approach to engaging their critical investors in their quarterly or annual results. These include:

- the largest investors by amount invested;
- the influential investors, who others take their lead from or who publish recommendations to others; and
- the wavering investors.

The company then arranges 'dialogue meetings' between the chief executive and/or financial director, along with the head of investor relations, with each key investor. These meetings start, not with a presentation, but by asking the investor:

- What would they like from the meeting? (*contracting*)
- What is their current policy, approach, and challenges in investing? (*listening*)
- What would be useful for them to hear about the performance of the company and its strategic plans going forward? (*exploring*)
- How would they like the company to work with them and communicate going forward? (*action*)
- Has this meeting has been helpful and how could such meetings be more helpful in the future? (*review*)

Using a coaching style with partner organizations and suppliers

When working in organizational partnerships, whether they are joint ventures, mergers or public sector partnerships, conflict often develops because both parties have not developed a clear joint endeavour and agenda. This can be done by jointly addressing the question:

> What is it we can achieve together that we cannot do apart?

Once having established a joint endeavour, the partner organizations can then work on agreeing key performance objectives and goals for their joint work, and then agree processes and protocols for working together. Sometimes, for complex partnerships of multiple organizations, this process can be coached by a skilled partnership coach or a joint facilitation team drawn from all partner organizations.

In their popular book *Getting to Yes*, Fisher and Ury (1991) outline a very useful model for ways of working with partner organizations. They propose a simple four-step process:

1. Separate the people from the problem
   - Clarify each other's perception of the situation
   - Recognize emotions
   - Communicate clearly
2. Focus on interests, not positions
   - Ask questions to explore interests
   - Talk about your own interests
3. Invent options for mutual gain
   - Brainstorm
   - Broaden options for mutual gain
4. Insist on using objective criteria
   - Fair standards
   - Fair procedures.

Coaching approach to engaging with regulators

Regulation of all organizations, whether in the private, public or civil society sector, has increased markedly in the last twenty years. Governments and the general public expect greater accountability and transparency from every organization and from those that lead them. Many organizations see their regulators as unwelcome, oppositional examiners that they need to fear or impress, and meeting with them an ordeal to be survived.

> When I was coaching the executive team of a large government department, they were about to undergo the annual follow-up to their initial capability review. This review had indicated a number of key areas that needed to be improved, and an action plan had been put into operation. The debate in the executive team was whether they should put together an impressive presentation, showing the progress that had been made and hiding the areas that had not improved, or be more open and honest. Those arguing for the former approach pointed out that if they were honest they would be seen less favourably than other departments, which would reflect badly on them as the executive leaders and this would be based on an unfair comparison. Those who argued for the latter pointed out that

> the weaknesses might emerge anyway, and it would be unsatisfying to get a good report based on what they would all know was 'spin'. Both sides were seeing the reviewers as audience and examiners to be impressed and feared. I asked them what they would do differently if they treated their regulators as friendly partners who, like them, cared about how to help the department become more effective and efficient? I also asked them to consider how they could get the most value out of the intelligence and outsider perspective of those visiting. This reframing led them to present both where they had made significant progress, as well as those areas they would like coaching from the assessors on how they could make more progress. This led to both parties leaving the meeting far more positively, and with added value to the next stage of the department's development.

Coaching in and with the communities in which the organization operates

Organizations often ignore the communities in which they operate and fail to see them as critical stakeholders. When something goes wrong locally, they discover too late that they have more local enemies than local allies. This is a process that can be seen in the relationship between some oil companies and those who live in territories in which the oil companies have been drilling. Corporations need positive relationships with their local communities. One way that some organizations have used coaching within the community is to ask staff to volunteer to provide coaching to local charities and community groups. It has been found that this has a number of benefits:

- It provides an appreciated service to the local groups.
- It increases staff skills, not only in coaching, but also in sensitively managing people and change processes in a very different setting; some managers have reported that this is the best learning and development in leadership they had undertaken.
- Staff return with a greater appreciation of their own work privilege, having seen staff in such agencies, often working longer hours for less pay and with far less support and internal resources.
- It builds stronger links between the company and its local community.
- It raises the positive profile of the organization.

One of the venture capital companies and one of the top four professional service firms I interviewed encourage their staff to become mentors for the Prince of Wales Trust, which supports young entrepreneurs and their entrepreneurial new businesses. They found that this involvement grew their staff skills; kept them in touch with how to engage young people from what is commonly called Generation Y (those born after 1980 and who grew up in the digital computerized society); and built a positive relationship with their possible future customers.

Those in the public sector have regularly to engage their local communities. Here a coaching style can help leaders radically change how they engage the public, with beneficial results. One public sector leader on the North West Employers Chief Executive Coaching programme reported how the training had helped him deal with difficult public meetings:

> I went along to what was set up as a 'lion's den' and I was much more consciously thinking about what people were saying and playing it back more. I was doing it with much more quality of listening and it went down really well.

Conclusion

In all these different examples we can see a similar pattern of moving from a 'tell and sell' presentation approach in which stakeholders are seen as 'other', to engaging stakeholders as a key part of the networked organization. The first step is understanding stakeholders' needs and interests, before exploring how to create a win–win–win relationship, for both parties and for their joint enterprise, including all the interests that the two parties share.

This seventh and final step in creating a coaching culture is where the internal organizational culture that has nurtured and adopted coaching interfaces with the external world. It is where a coaching culture can make a significant difference to the 'lived brand' of the organization (how it engages daily with all its stakeholders) and how the organization is perceived and rated by its customers, suppliers, partners, investors, and its surrounding communities. The positive difference that can be created in these perceptions drives a good deal of organizational performance and organizational value as well as mitigating potential business risk.

PART 3
Integration and depth

11 How to get all the elements working together and aligned to the 'relational value chain'

Introduction

Most of the organizations we have studied are pioneers and none would claim that they have a full-fledged coaching culture. Indeed, we should avoid the trap of believing that this journey is linear and that there is a destination. It is a perpetual journey, with new ways of continuously improving the quality of relationships and conversations within the organization and between the organization and its wider system of stakeholders. However, by looking at the range of leading practice in the seven steps outlined, we can begin to envision an organization with all seven steps flourishing, aligned, and creating a synergistic impact on the organization and its development.

Different pathways through the steps

I have outlined the seven steps in a particular order, based on the most common sequence that organizations appear to undertake. However, this is not a blueprint and there are different sequences that some organizations have used, with the order being context specific. The following are a few of the many possible routes through the steps.

The sequence as presented. In this most common of sequences adopted, the organization starts with putting in place quality external provision. If done well, this creates a large pool of senior executives who have experienced and understand the personal benefits of coaching, and have a role model of how to engage in a coaching style. The danger is that it builds dependency on expensive external resources, and coaching remains something carried out externally behind closed doors and not strongly linked back to the organization

Starting with an internal coaching service. A few organizations have chosen to start not with external coaches, but by building the internal coaching capability, so that internal coaches become the norm and are strongly valued at all levels. Some organizations have found that recruiting and developing a small pool of internal coaches that work full time creates a more integrated coaching service, and that this group can best decide when an external coach is specifically needed.

Starting by building a coaching approach and coaching skills into all management and leadership training and development. Sometimes the initiative comes from the head of learning and development who, in reviewing all the organization's training and development activities and expenditure, can see the benefits of ensuring that all training activities have more of a coaching style of delivery, and that coaching skills should be a key component of all management and leadership programmes. This, as we can see in the case study later in the chapter on Phoenix, can create a shared new language and approach right across the organization. However, there is a danger that the coaching will be widely but thinly spread, with a great deal of brief skill and performance coaching, but little coaching that focuses on long-term development and transformation of people's ways of being.

The six main traps and pitfalls

In my many interviews with coaching sponsors, coach managers, external coaches and supervisors, internal coaches and supervisors, and those leading the journey to creating a coaching culture, I often heard stories describing what had gone wrong or become problematic on the journey. Sometimes, the stories I heard were narratives about setbacks and challenges that were overcome. Sometimes, however, they were stories of how the initial good work and investment had been undermined by a major problem that had not yet been overcome.

In reviewing all my notes I could see a pattern emerging of some of the most common setbacks. I list them below, not in the order of their prevalence, but in the order they are often encountered on the journey.

1. Not building a wide enough sponsorship group

In two organizations, the development of coaching activities had occurred very quickly, through a combination of a very senior sponsor and a determined coach organizer. However, the senior sponsor had not managed to enrol his colleagues in supporting these efforts, or even in understanding the benefits. Hence when this senior sponsor left, the coaching activities gradually diminished and all progress was halted.

It is important to ensure that coaching activities have a wide sponsorship from all parts of the business, and that coach managers equip their senior sponsors with regular updates, reviews, and evaluation to keep their colleagues informed and supporting the activities. In Chapter 13, I explore further how to evaluate coaching activities at all stages of the journey, including how this can be used to continue to get the interest and active support of senior sponsors.

2. The coaching remains an HR initiative

I believe that HR has a central and critical role in developing, implementing, and sustaining the coaching culture and the coaching strategy. However, there is a danger if coaching activities appear to be owned by, and identified with, HR. This can cause line managers to see coaching as only being about the 'softer' aspects of the business and about individual and personal development. For a coaching culture to flourish, it needs to be seen to be linked to business success and performance improvement, and for this to happen it needs to be seen to have the active support of senior executives, line management, and the finance section.

I worked with a senior executive team who had a habit of splitting what they termed the 'hard stuff' (bottom-line financial results, task efficiency, etc.) from the 'soft stuff' (people, relationships, and emotions). I told them that financial results were indeed the hard stuff, but that coaching dealt with the 'harder stuff'! They asked me what I meant, and I said:

> Having the difficult conversations inside the organization that will shift performance and developing the commercially beneficial external relationships was indeed harder than cutting impersonal costs or launching new products, because it involved more aspects of ourselves. Only by improving relationships internally and externally will you shift perceptions of the organization, create customer/client and stakeholder commitment, grow partnerships, and deliver shared value.

3. Failure to retain key staff

I interviewed a number of coaching and HR managers, particularly in the public sector, who had suffered severe setbacks through key staff, who had a lot of drive, political influence or coaching expertise, leaving either through employee cutbacks or because they wanted to work as a freelance coach or join a coaching consultancy. New initiatives are often started by charismatic entrepreneurs. These people are often more motivated to start new endeavours than they are to sustain them and so always have a higher than average tendency to move on. If these people leave before they have built the sustaining mechanisms into the fabric of the service, there is always some vulnerability to ongoing development. Coaching communities need to attend to their own succession planning from the outset.

There is also a danger that having trained a number of good internal staff, several of them may want to move on to roles where they can utilize their new found skills to a greater extent. The Legal Services Commission of the British government worked hard to develop an internal coaching community and trained twenty-four coaching champions, with ILM accreditation. Three years later, Elizabeth Crosse, who managed the service, reported that only two of the twenty-four remained. This was partly due to the merger of the Legal Services Commission with the Department of Justice and partly due to the reduction in staff numbers in the department. Some trained internal coaches had left to work for other government departments, taking their skills with them. However, given that one of the key objectives of their coaching strategy was to 'retain high performing staff as we move through change', they realized they had not done enough to retain their high-performing internal coaches.

The retention of coaches can be aided by ensuring regular continuing personal and professional development, supervision, and review for all coaches (see Chapter 12). It is important to ensure that they are receiving good career planning sessions with senior management so that their coaching skills are also being developed into wider leadership responsibilities, including a shared view about how these might be used elsewhere in the organization through promotion.

4. Believing that having a lot of coaching activity is sufficient to create a coaching culture

A number of organizations have focused their coaching activities on building their coaching resources, such as building a pool of external and internal coaches, and ensuring a lot of coaching was happening, and then failed to move to the later steps in the journey. A lot of coaching activity does not create a coaching culture, and it is only when the coaching activity is focused on delivering organizational learning, performance improvement, and changed relationships internally and externally, that the organization starts to deliver the real value. These organizations had put in place the inputs without supporting the outputs and outcomes that would deliver the value.

5. Not ensuring quality assurance and management of the service

One coaching manager said to me, 'the first three years we were just focused on the amount of coaching we could get to happen. This is what we reported on to the senior managers. Only now have we started to think, not just about the quantity of what we are doing, but about the quality'. The quality of coaching is not just about recruiting the right coaches. It is also about ensuring that all coaches (external and internal) are having good quality supervision and continuous development. This is the subject of the next chapter.

Quality coaching does not just come from the coach. There are several other key factors that positively impact the quality of the coaching:

- the coachee needs to be motivated and clear on the benefits they can obtain from coaching;
- the coach's approach, experience, and skills need to be well matched to the needs of the coachee;
- the relationship that develops between the two parties;
- how this relationship is linked to the wider organization, through: three- and four-way contracting and review; 360-degree feedback; and connection with organizational initiatives and strategy, etc.

6. Failure to evaluate

Many organizations will support coaching for a while based on the enthusiastic support of a few champions and on personal testimony of individual benefits. However, sooner or later other, more sceptical executives will start to ask the question, 'How do we know that this is a useful investment of time and money?' Or, 'How are we measuring the return on investment?' Before you reach this point, it is important to build in rigorous evaluation of all aspects of the coaching activities and coaching culture. As one coaching manager put it:

> If we don't start to measure the benefits of our service, in ways sympathetic to the spirit of what we are trying to do, then they will start to measure us in ways we may not think are sensible.

Ways to evaluate the benefits of coaching and crafting a coaching culture will be addressed in Chapter 13.

How the coaching culture links to other aspects of culture change

As explored in Chapter 3, the seven steps to creating a coaching culture need to be linked to the wider organizational culture change, which, in turn, is linked to the strategy and mission of the organization.

The following case study of working with the elderly care profession in Sweden provides an illustration of a number of the different ingredients of the culture change infrastructure coming together and being aligned with changing the culture and effectiveness of an area of work in the public sector. Rüddi Porsgaard shows there is a clear attempt to create a coaching culture that will change the organizational climate, staff morale, the service to the elderly people of the region, and deliver better economic efficiency.

Case study: Phoenix: development of leadership and team culture in elderly care
Project Phoenix is a Swedish project, funded by the European Social Fund between July 2009 and April 2011. The idea for the project was developed by Britt-Marie Högberg (leader in elderly care, Lundby, Gothenburg) and Rüddi Porsgaard (chief executive of Strandska). Britt-Marie wanted her colleagues to learn from a coaching approach as part of efforts to introduce the salutogenic approach in geriatric care, which she recognized would require a major culture change in the organization. The salutogenic approach focuses on the factors that support health and positive personal and social functioning in elderly clients. Several factors had led to this need for a cultural change:

- The view of the service by society and the staff themselves no longer matched the type of service provided. It was more common to label elderly care as a 'housewife service', as opposed to the more accurate label, 'rehabilitation and development of the elderly'.
- It was necessary to improve and develop the communication skills of the employees.
- There was a need to explore new career opportunities for employees working in the field, as well as finding innovative ways of attracting both men and women for the different tasks and assignments.
- The economic climate of greater demand and the same limited resources required new, more efficient practices that could shorten the period of rehabilitation and at the same time create a more healthy work environment for the staff.
- High absence rates as well as disciplinary problems, due to lack of skills in communication, were noted in some teams.

The adoption of a salutogenic approach to the elderly also required creating a salutogenic approach to developing the staff – an approach that would promote the staff's social and psychological health, well-being, and positivity. Thus, the challenge was to implement a process of change and development that would result in a salutogenic organization with a coaching culture, within eighteen months. Another purpose was to improve staff relationships, morale, and performance, as well as introduce better working methods.

As part of the development it was important for all staff to learn how to use the correct type of coaching and communication skills to:

- prevent problems in the workplace;
- resolve issues before they mushroomed into bigger problems;
- create development in the team and for clients;
- empathize and listen to co-workers and clients;
- be more efficient at achieving goals and group tasks;
- achieve objectives and group efficiency in a better way.

It was important that all employees realized that the project was not just about acquiring coaching skills, but also about changing internal relationships, improving communication, and team functioning, in service of better care for the elderly clients as well as a better work climate. The members of the team and their team leader also needed to appreciate how the team's internal learning and team dynamics had an impact on employee performance. These three parts needed to come together in each team to develop a better understanding of how team culture, team structure, and the team's internal learning could make a difference to how the team performed and contributed to efficient elderly care.

The culture in elderly care had, in some cases, been built on a more directive and controlling leadership style, with little employee autonomy and development. There was now a desire for a culture that could provide greater development, a learning environment, and the possibility for employees to be free in their way of working, but still with responsibility. To achieve a lasting cultural change in the organizations, we realized that we would need to work with the leaders and employees in parallel. Both employees and leaders were offered the same training programme with some minor adjustments. We also realized that if we were to achieve this cultural change, it would require not only the development of leaders, managers, and front line staff, but also developing the 'space between them' (i.e. the relationship between managers and employees). The cultural change begins with our relationships within the organization and how these relationships take expression in the communication between employees, between employees and managers, and between leaders and their superiors.

It is difficult for employees to implement political directives if they do not fully understand the implications and content of those directives. This can hinder their performance when meeting with clients.

Design

During the project, 90 managers, 650 employees, and 50 teams were trained in a coaching approach, and developing communication. All leaders and union counsellors in the workplace were trained in coaching and team coaching (seven days). All employees were trained in coaching skills (two days). Each team was offered two places on a basic coaching programme (five days), and one or two employees were offered training for people who would consider an alternative career as internal developers on a professional coach training (18 days), culminating in examinations and accreditation as a certified coach.

In addition to individual training in coaching skills, all teams were given three and a half days of team development spread over a six-month period. This team development involved working on the team's internal and external relationships and how to improve communication.

Results

A pilot study had shown that just one hour a week of coaching for the staff led to increased satisfaction in their work with the elderly and a decrease in treatment time. The coaching approach had a positive impact on the elderly's autonomy and they expressed a more positive perception of the care they received.

The project showed how a coaching approach not only developed the staff's relationships with one another in the team but also was a tool to develop the insights, communication, and relationship with the elderly clients and with others in their team. Many of the participants stated that relationships had been strengthened and that they had become more satisfied and happier in their work. We noticed that leaders were more able to meet and develop their employees instead of managing them as difficult staff members. Many leaders and group members have stated that there is much less conflicts and that it was easer to prevent and solve conflicts after the programme.

The results of the parallel education are an equal relationship between employees and managers where they can respond to each other instead of reacting under pressure in exposed situations. When staff can communicate in a developing way, they can better execute decisions and handle pedagogical challenges that sometimes occur between care takers and their relatives when changes are made.

> It was a very good choice we made when we joined the project. We communicate in an entirely different way today; we work well together, towards common goals. We have set the ground rules in our groups which we work with daily and that have created a better working environment.
>
> (Lise Andreasson, leader, Tuve-Säve, Gothenburg)

Other leaders reported in the evaluation feedback:

> 'People talk *to* each other instead of talking *about* each other.'
> 'The employees have gone from a feeling of working as a maid to a feeling of working with rehabilitation.'
> 'The employees show more pride in their work and their satisfaction is noticeable.'
> 'I don't need to check on the team as often as before, the team members solve situations themselves, and I as a leader have more

> time for strategic work or to use the time for group learning instead of conflict resolution.'
>
> 'The work climate has gradually become better and more pleasant. We have a good team spirit, but individual pride – you learn simple little tricks that make a big impact.'
>
> The project has shown that developing a coaching culture can improve the leader's and employees' communication skills, promote better efficiency and health, for both staff members and their clients, and combined with the salutogenic approach, can create a culutre based on living values that are important for our society.

Most organizational culture change programmes are easier to initiate than to sustain. However well they are designed upfront, they need to be adapted, made more flexible, and often redesigned in the light of what emerges in the process. Only when you try and change a culture do you discover more about the deeper levels of that culture that are obstacles to it changing.

A successful culture change cannot be designed by the senior leadership alone, or by the HR department, or by external consultants, although all of these have their role to play. Each party will only see the wider system from their privileged and limited perspective. Culture change needs to be a collaborative, iterative, and adaptive process that reviews itself at each stage of the process, learning more as it proceeds.

The 'relational value chain' and the role of coaching

The seven steps of the coaching culture need to be linked to the wider organizational strategic and culture change processes, and those leading the initiatives need to be able to articulate the wider business case and business change. One of the most effective frameworks for doing this is the concept of the 'relational value chain', which is a model I have developed for how organizations create increased value by differentiating how they do business with all their stakeholders.

It has been recognized for some time that businesses should have a strong focus on managing their complete value chain. This is a product- or service-based value chain that reaches back through the organization's complete supplier base and forward to how the products and services of the company are used by its customers, and its customers' customers. There have been many advances in streamlining the complete value chain and driving greater efficiencies through every stage of the process and between the stages. These include: Total Quality Management, Business Re-engineering, Lean Processes and Design, and Six Sigma. Such work, although pioneered in sectors such as car manufacturing (Toyota and Lean Manufacturing, Unipart and Six Sigma), has also been applied in the public sector when looking at, for example, the complete patient pathway in the health service, an integrated approach to supporting those on welfare back into work, and the processing of passports.

Far less has been written about the relational value chain. Many companies have recognized that it has become more difficult to differentiate their product or service either by quality or price, as having a high-quality product at a low price is a prerequisite for simply remaining competitive in a market. Technical advantage also provides less of a sustainable competitive advantage than it once did. Technical innovation by one organization can very quickly be learnt, copied, and improved on by another, as can process improvements. The global Internet and other technological changes have led to a revolution in the speed and transparency of communication, which has transformed the speed and accessibility of knowledge transfer of every kind.

Thus increasingly organizations have been focusing on how they can differentiate through 'how' they do business – the quality of their relationships with their customers, suppliers, and other stakeholders. In working with a number of organizations in manufacturing, professional services, and the public and civil society sectors, I have developed 'the relational value chain', which works in parallel with the product or service value chain.

The value of an organization lies significantly in the positive difference it creates for its customers and stakeholders. This, in turn, is strongly linked to the positive perception these customers and stakeholders have of the organization, which influences: the stakeholders' desire to continue to invest; partners to partner; suppliers to supply; and the customer or client to buy from and use the services of the organization. This, in turn, influences the value of an organization as represented by its share price and the price it might be sold for, or in the public sector and civil society, by its capacity to survive and grow.

Stakeholders' perceptions are now affected significantly by their experience of the organization in the thousands of daily encounters and through ongoing relationships. I have termed this 'the lived brand' of the company – how it lives, breathes, and behaves, as it engages with its wider system. The lived brand cannot be controlled by the organizational leaders, or managed in the same way that the marketing brand is managed, but is dependent on the moment-by-moment actions of everyone who works for the organization.

One of the main determinants of how employees engage with their customers and stakeholders is how they themselves are treated and managed by their direct managers and, to a lesser extent, the organizational leaders. This is not just how well the managers manage and the leaders lead, but is also the organizational culture. Employees imbibe the culture of the organization from the moment they first walk through the door. The culture becomes part of the taken-for-granted, unnoticed ways of thinking, feeling, and doing in the

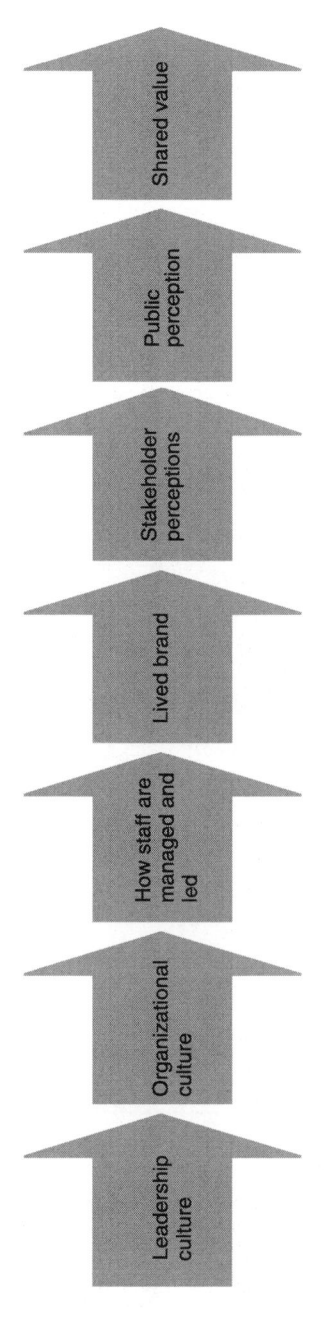

Figure 11.1 The relational value chain.

Figure 11.2 The relational value chain: the contribution of coaching.

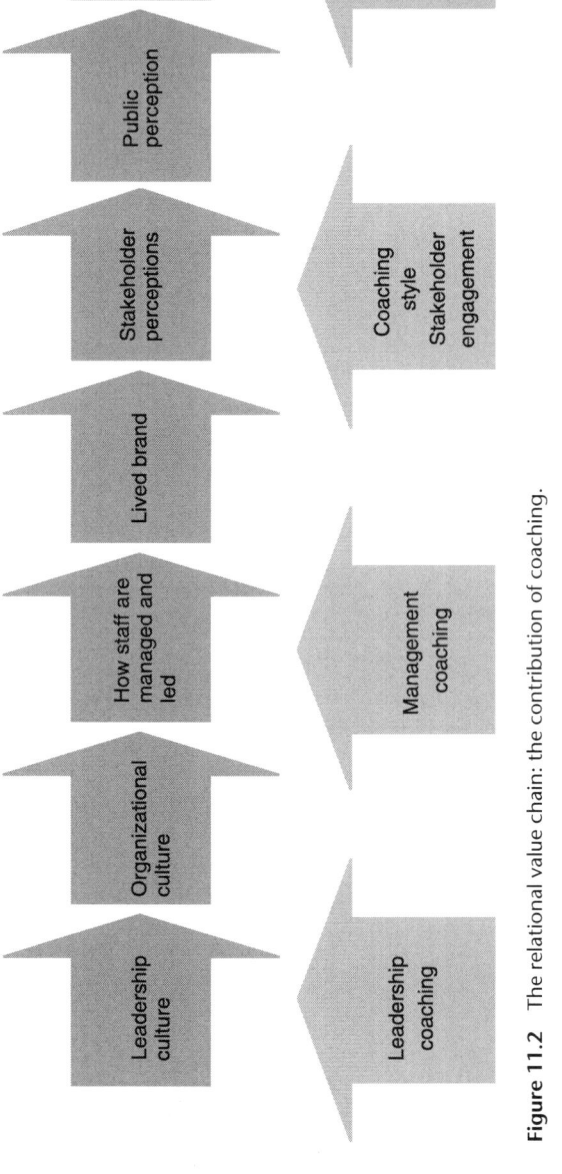

organization. Once new employees have worked in the organization for three months of more, they too consider this way of being as natural and stop being aware of the organizational culture. One of the main determinants of the organizational culture is the leadership culture – not just what the leaders decide or communicate, but how they engage and relate both internally and externally.

Coaching can make an important contribution to this relational value chain in a number of significant stages (see Figure 11.2).

Conclusion

In this chapter, I have looked at different pathways through the seven steps of the coaching culture journey, the traps and pitfalls that might be encountered on the way, and the need to see the journey as part of a bigger organizational development framework to improve the relational value chain of the organization.

Underpinning the seven steps are the three pillars of a clear coaching strategy linked to the business strategy, a coaching journey linked to a culture change journey for the whole organization, and a coaching infrastructure that supports and integrates the multiple coaching activities. However, the seven steps and the three pillars are necessary but not sufficient. They will ensure a great deal of coaching activity, aligned to the business objectives and organizational development. To achieve a real and lasting benefit from all the coaching activities, the organization needs to attend to the depth, range, and quality of the coaching that happens. This need for expanding the depth of coaching and ongoing quality improvement requires supervision and continuous personal and professional development as well as rigorous evaluation of the coaching and its impact, and these are the subjects of the next two chapters.

12 Expanding the depth and improving the quality of coaching activities: supervision and continuous personal and professional development

Introduction

In this chapter, I start by looking at the depth and effectiveness of coaching before looking at three key aspects of quality improvement for all organizations that are using coaching:

- continuing personal and professional development for all coaches, leaders, and managers using coaching skills;
- regular good quality supervision for all internal and external coaches;
- regular reviews of the coaching service and its contribution to the wider organization and its development.

I then show why an organization cannot ensure continual learning and supervision by itself, but needs to be part of a wider movement across organizations and coaching bodies to create a vibrant learning coaching profession.

Deepening the coaching

In Hawkins and Smith (2006), we presented a model of the coaching continuum to describe the range and the depth of coaching whereby different types of coaching required increasing capability and capacity from the coach and a corresponding depth in the coaching relationship. The focus of *skills coaching* is on growing the competence of the coachee in specific areas of their work. *Performance coaching* develops the coachee's capability of using their competence, at the right time and in the right way, to improve their own performance, and that of their team and the organization. Both skills coaching and performance coaching can be delivered by line managers who have developed the necessary coaching skills and style to engage their staff.

Development coaching focuses not just on improving the performance of the coachee in their current role, but also helping them to develop the capabilities and capacities they will need to progress in future roles. This form of coaching is harder for the line manager to deliver as they have more of a vested interest in the current performance, less awareness of wider leadership capacities, and are normally less well trained in developmental coaching. This form of coaching will often be linked to individuals attending leadership development programmes and can be delivered by good quality internal coaches or external coaches.

Transformational coaching focuses on helping clients transform how they think, feel, and behave, when working on their issues, in such a way that they will also create a 'knock-on shift' in the wider system. Hawkins and Smith (2010) distinguish four key elements of such coaching:

1. *Shifting the meaning scheme.* The ability to help clients change their 'meaning schemes' (specific beliefs, attitudes, and emotional reactions) during the coaching session, which leads to a 'perspective transformation' for the client.
2. *Working on multiple levels at the same time.* To effect this change with the client, the coach needs to be able to work on multiple levels at the same time (that is, to attend to the physical, psychological, emotional, and purposive elements and how they combine in the present situation). The change in perspective has to be 'embodied' (i.e. the coachee needs to be able to think, feel, *and* do differently) for it to be truly transformational.
3. *Shift in the room.* Transformational coaching therefore focuses strongly on freeing the coachee's 'stuck' perspective within the session, live in the room. The process by which the coach helps the client experience an integrated transformation of perspective is termed 'creating a shift in the room'. We use a method of first matching and then mismatching the coachee to create the transformational shift.
4. *Four levels of engagement.* The change in perspective comes through a change in the coachee's assumptions, values, and beliefs about the issue they brought. Transformational coaches use the 'four levels of engagement' model to map the connection of these assumptions to the feelings that drive the behaviours, which then generate the specific responses an executive is trying to modify (see Figure 12.1).

These four levels of coaching can be used by coaches, manager, and leaders working with the other forms of coaching, but then they will be in service of shifting skill, performance or developing greater capacity. In transformational coaching, the four levels are engaged in the service of helping the individual shift their action logic (Torbert, 2004), 'cognitive frame of

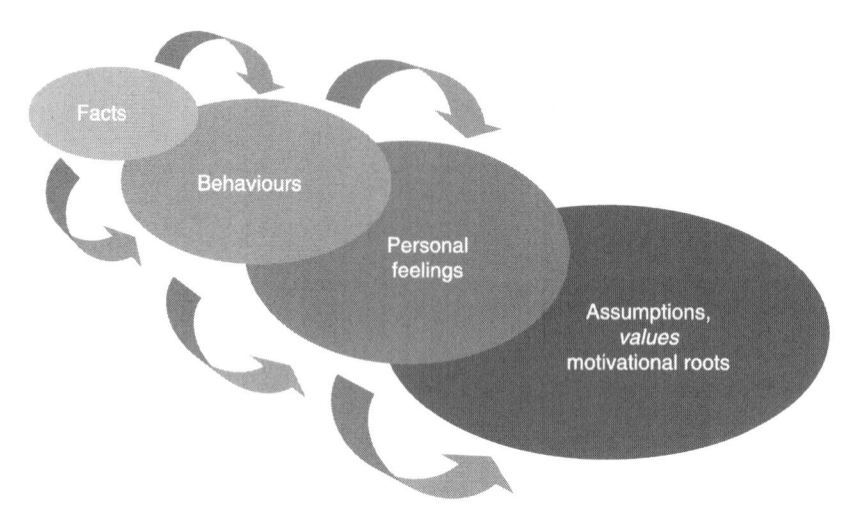

Figure 12.1 Four levels of engagement.

reference' (Laske, 2003), emotional patterns, relational capacity (Hawkins, 2011b), and ethical maturity (Hawkins, 2011b). With this form of coaching, there is also an emphasis on the coaching moving beyond new understanding, insight, awareness, and good intention, to embodied learning and change live in the room. This involves not just asking the coachee what they are planning to do, but asking them to try out the new behaviour in a 'fast-forward rehearsal'.

As executives and leaders face greater complexity, ambiguity, challenge, and demands to be more inspirational and motivational, it is important that coaching provides greater depth of engagement and more profound and sustainable change. This means that coaches need to be supported in their own constant reflection and development, and their capacity to engage their coaches at all four levels of engagement. Although it is likely that external coaches will provide transformational coaching, I would contend that in a coaching culture there should be a continuous effort to increase the depth of engagement in all types of coaching. To this end, transformational coaching approaches can be used in all forms of coaching.

Continuous personal and professional development

Throughout this book I have argued that continuous personal and professional development are essential elements for all those practising coaching, as well as those who attempt to lead or manage with a coaching style approach. Continuing professional development (CPD) with updates on new skills and methods in coaching is useful but not sufficient. At the heart of effective coaching is the coaching relationship (de Hahn, 2008; Hawkins and Schwenk, 2010) and the most important coaching tool that any coach has is him or herself. Instead of CPD we need to focus on CPPD (continuous personal and professional development), where the development focuses on expanding the emotional, ethical, and cognitive capacities of the coach, manager, and leader (Hawkins, 2011b). Together with my colleague Danny Chesterman, in 2006 we conducted research for the Teacher Support Network into the importance of CPPD for teachers. The report was called 'Every Teacher Matters' and argued that for teachers to grow their effectiveness, they need constant opportunities for personal growth and reflective practice.

The coaching profession needs a similar report, 'Every Coach Matters'. Basic training can inspire and motivate. Early supervised and supported practice can lay the foundations for good practice, but without attention to personal and professional development, it is only too common for our practice to slide into uncreative patterns, limited responses, and stuck relationships.

Many of the organizations that I interviewed had arranged regular half-day development sessions for their internal and occasionally for their external coaches. Some organizations had made these mandatory for their coaches. The best practice that emerged was to ensure that these sessions had a good and integrated balance of both professional knowledge and skill development, together with personal development of capabilities and capacities. A number of organizations did this by having master classes with leading coach practitioners who would present an aspect of coaching, demonstrating a way of working with it live in the session, and then arrange practical coaching experience with the participants using the presented approach live in the room. At other times, the experiential and personal learning was provided by small groups supervising each other on current coaching relationships, using the new perspective.

Supervision for ensuring quality

There has been much debate in the last few years on the place of supervision in coaching. In 2006, in the research carried out in the UK by Bath Consultancy Group for CIPD (Hawkins and Schwenk, 2006), we received responses from 120 organizations and 530 individual coaches. The results of this survey showed that 88 per cent of organizers of coaching and 86 per cent of coaches believed that coaches should have regular ongoing supervision for their coaching.

However, only 44 per cent of coaches who responded were currently receiving regular ongoing supervision and only 23 per cent of the organizations provided regular ongoing coaching supervision. Even among the minority of coaches who were receiving supervision, 58 per cent had only started receiving supervision within the previous two years. The survey and the subsequent focus groups and organizational best practice studies showed high advocacy for the importance of supervision, but practice lagged some way behind. Our experience is that in most other countries coaching supervision is even less well established, although there is a growing acceptance of its importance across Europe (Bachkirova et al., 2011).

The reasons for the gap between advocacy and practice include the shortage of trained and skilled supervisors (the first full training course specifically for coaching supervision in the UK commenced in December 2003). Other factors include cost and the lack of clarity concerning the requirement for supervision from the professional bodies and employers.

There is now a marked growth in both the requirement for coaching supervision by organizational buyers and in the number of coaches partaking. In best practice studies of organizations (Hawkins and Schwenk, 2006), some of the notable quotes from organizational heads of coaching included:

> To open one's work to scrutiny is important best practice in any helping activity. If you are going to invest in coaches in the workplace, this is an essential part of it – it is not an optional exercise.
> (Barbara Picheta, Head of Coaching, PricewaterhouseCoopers UK)

> I would expect coaches to have supervision as part of their continuous professional development and I would not employ a coach who did not have supervision.
> (Shaun Lincoln, Centre for Excellence in Leadership)

In the last two years in the UK, the number of training courses in coaching supervision has grown rapidly, as have the number of conference workshops on the subject. Coaching supervision training has also begun in a number of other countries.

Coaching supervision can be defined as:

> The process by which a Coach with the help of a Supervisor, can attend to understanding better both the Client system and themselves as part of the Client–Coach system, and by so doing transform their work and develop their craft.
> (Hawkins and Smith, 2006: 147)

Although there is still contention about whether supervision is an essential requirement for all coaches, there is a general acceptance that regular review of one's work by another professional is not only a key aspect of professional quality assurance, but also a key aspect of continuing professional and personal development.

> Two organizations that I interviewed (BBC and NHSI) had both invested in developing their own internal supervisors. The NHSI (the National Health Service Institute for Innovation and Improvement) has now run two training programmes with Bath Consultancy Group, in coaching supervision, each for ten to twelve senior internal coaches and are planning a third. Those on these courses were drawn from different regions of the country so as to provide a spread of local supervisory support. Those who attended were not only positive about the coaching supervision skills they had developed, but also how learning to supervise other coaches had increased the depth and range of their own coaching capacities. The programme involved two three-day modules as well as the participants undertaking 25 hours of supervision of coaches in the health service, with five hours of supervision on their supervision. They then had the opportunity to complete the rest of the full Bath Consultancy Group Coaching Supervision training certificate on the open programme.

Supervision for managers using a coaching style clearly needs to be different from that required for more specialist coaches. Maxwell (2011) advocates that the supervision of a manager's coaching of their staff, should be addressed in their own line management conversations with the person they directly report to. However, as suggested in Chapter 9, this supervision needs at times to be supplemented by peer support and supervision, possibly in action learning sets or coaching practicum groups, or by their the opportunity to take issues to supervision with an experienced internal or external coach.

Regular review of the coaching service and its contribution to the development of the organization

While CPPD and supervision can ensure constant learning for individual coaches and the collective community of coaches, it is also important that the coaching organization and the wider organization are also engaged in cycles of learning and development.

In the next chapter, I explore evaluation and research methods that can be used to look at both the quality of the coaching practices as well as their impact on individual, team, and organizational performance. What is important for developing the quality and depth of coaching practice is that the evaluation and research is used for all the providers of coaching, and that coaching style leaders and managers reflect on their work so as to deepen and improve it.

Some of the organizations interviewed reported that they sent copies of the evaluation reports to their external and internal coaches. Others made presentations at development sessions. This information sharing can be useful, but in itself does not provide an impetus to quality improvement and can, at worst, just lead to defensiveness and/or complacency. Feedback data delivered in a 'tell and sell' style outside of dialogue and active inquiry will always tend to create an air of judgement and potential defensiveness.

The impact of evaluation or reviews on the coaching provider is more developmental if the research and review are carried out using a more collaborative action research style (Reason and Bradbury, 2000). This entails involving the internal and external coaches in consultation prior to the review or evaluation, in looking at what questions about their individual and collective practice they would like the research and/or review to address, and what they would like to learn from the process. Then, when the results are presented back, it is important to once again ask the coaches about the learning they want from the evaluation and to actively engage them with what has emerged.

Establishing an appropriate learning profession

In Chapter 1, I highlighted that the development of an appropriate, integrated, and learning profession is one of the major challenges for coaching. Buyers of coaching have frequently commented on how the confusion in terminology and definitions is further exacerbated by the current professional fragmentation, which includes:

- a number of competing professional bodies with different standards and approaches;
- a proliferation of terms and their uses;
- a wide variety of routes to becoming an accredited professional;
- a wide variety of training programmes from very short courses to doctorates.

There is a continuing need for the profession to create learning across professional bodies, different training organizations, researchers, practitioners, and teachers. There have been useful developments in creating facilitated forums of different organizations sharing their journey in creating a coaching culture. Both the Association for Professional Executive Coaching and Supervision and the European Mentoring and Coaching Council organize such forums in the UK. At best these can become a form of organizational peer supervision, where organizations help each other to develop their organizational practice. Increasingly, coaching conferences are not just dominated by external coaches presenting their methodology, but a rich mix of internal and external coaches, line mangers, and coaching organizers all learning from each other. However, there is still a long way to go to create a learning profession, where the profession has moved beyond trying to regulate its members' practice and inducting newcomers into best practice (although both are important), to providing ways in which the profession can constantly evolve and learn from the new practice that is emerging at the leading edge of practice in organizations.

I have written elsewhere (Hawkins and Shohet, 2006: 206) about how supervision can become an important aspect of this learning profession:

> If we are to create learning professions that constantly renew their cultures, then supervision needs to become the 'learning lungs' that assist the professional body in its learning, development and cultural evolution. Supervision needs to be a place of co-creative and generative thinking where new learning is being forged for the clients, coach, supervisor and for the profession.

Conclusion

To sustain a coaching culture it is essential to constantly attend to the quality of the coaching at all levels and from all forms of supplier (internal, external, and line management). This requires both continuous personal and professional development for all those carrying out coaching, as well as professional supervision for internal and external coaches. Indeed, those with the difficult job of managing the coaching service and being responsible for leading the journey towards a coaching culture also need some form of professional supervision, as it is hard to see the culture change when you are closely involved and working within it. The continuous development of coaching leaders and managers can also be greatly enhanced by attending conferences and learning forums where they can exchange learning and review with other organizations also on the journey.

13 Evaluation, research, and the return on investment from creating a coaching culture

Introduction

Coaches, coach managers, organizations, and the wider population of coach researchers need to focus not just on making a positive difference for individuals and organizations, but also on demonstrating that this is happening through building evaluation measures into every stage of coaching. These measures need to show the outputs and outcomes for the individual coachee, team, organization, and the wider system of stakeholders.

Most of the literature on evaluation, including Clutterbuck and Megginson's (2005) very thorough work, stops at Step 5 in my model of creating a coaching culture, where the evaluation focuses on the behavioural changes in the organization's employees. Normally, this requires measuring 'actual behaviours' against the 'espoused behaviours' in the company's core values, leadership qualities, manager competencies, and so on. The danger is that even though the behaviours might be 'nice ones to have', the link between the espoused behaviours and organizational performance may be illusory, since at this stage the evaluation is only focusing on the *outputs of behaviour in staff and not the outcomes of business performance*.

There is a salutary lesson from the car retail sector where there was, for many years, a major emphasis on customer satisfaction, with dealerships putting a lot of effort into measuring customer satisfaction and trying to outperform their competitors in this area. However, later research showed there was very little correlation between high levels of customer satisfaction soon after purchase, and the number of customers who bought their next car from the same dealer. It was only when the dealerships moved from measuring customer satisfaction (output) to measuring customer retention (outcome) that they began to develop an evaluation system that could support value generation across both a wider stakeholder group and over time.

The other evaluation trap is to measure short-term behaviour shifts and long-term financial performance and suggest that there is some causative link between them, without in any way researching or validating the connection.

Research in coaching is still in its infancy, and most of the focus to date has been on studying the coaching process, with very little rigorous research on outcome benefits, beyond those reported by the coaches. I thus start by looking at how evaluation can be built into each step of the coaching culture journey, and then tackle the larger issues of research and return on investment.

Evaluation at each step of the coaching culture journey

How an organization evaluates its coaching culture is likely to change as it progresses through the steps described in earlier chapters.

1. The organization employs coaches for some of its executives

At this stage of the journey, as I showed in Chapter 4, the work of many organizations is to move from different executives and parts of the organization personally hiring their own coaches to having a more integrated and planned approach. A key part of this structuring of the coaching provision is to organize standard processes of obtaining feedback, after the completion of every coaching assignment.

The feedback collected from coachees needs to cover the following important areas:

1. *Inputs*
    - Your name, role and time in current position.
    - Who did you have your coaching from?
    - How many sessions? How long? Over what period?
    - What was your and your manager's starting objectives or goals for the coaching?
    - What other learning and development processes was your coaching linked to, if any?
2. *Outputs*
    - What progress did you make on each of these objectives?
    - What difference has this made in terms of your work?
3. *Outcomes*
    - List any differences achieved in your work and in your team as a result of the coaching.

- How will you further the development you have started in this coaching?

4. *Feedback on the coach*
    - How would you rate your coach on a scale from 1 to 5 (5 = extremely effective, 4 = very effective, 3 = effective, 2 = helpful but not really effective, 1 = unhelpful)?
    - Who in the organization would you recommend to receive help from this coach?
    - How would you describe the coach's style and method?
    - What three words would you use to describe the coaching relationship?

If there has been three-way contracting with the involvement of a more senior manager at the beginning, middle, and end of the coaching assignment, then parallel feedback can be collected from the manager as well.

The aims of this feedback and evaluation process as outlined in Chapter 5 are to:

- help the coachee explore how they continue their learning and development after the coaching has ended, and link the development from their coaching to other forms of learning on and off the job;
- help the coach learn what has been most and least successful, and how they can increase their added value to other clients in this particular organization and beyond;
- help the line manager continue to support and develop the coachee;
- help the coaching service to both continue to develop its own service and to provide data that can be used anonymously in the on-going evaluation of coaching in the organization.

The compilation of such data then allows the coach manager to regularly review which executives are reporting the most benefit from being coached, and what factors in terms of length of session, frequency and style of coaching seem to affect the benefit. The coach manager can, in this way, receive regular feedback on each external coach. It would be wrong to judge any coach solely on one piece of feedback from a coachee. There will always be coaching relationships that do not work effectively, even those involving the most successful coaches.

It is important to decide whether this information will be treated confidentially, or whether it will be shared with the coach. On balance, I believe it is best if there is support for a culture of maximum openness and transparency, and the client is encouraged to share their feedback directly with the coach. Such information can also be used by the coaching manager to review feedback about the external coach. Often a coaching manager will do this, not after every assignment, but after every two or three assignments when it is possible to look at emerging patterns. The exception to this would be when there is a particular difficulty, such as a complaint about one of the coaches.

Some organizations I interviewed also have a structured form for the coach to complete. This can allow the coach to comment on any issues about how the coaching was set up and about processes that enabled or disabled the coaching from being at its most effective. Thus the coachee is giving feedback on the coach and the coach on management of the process. When devising and using such a form it is important that it allows the coach to preserve the appropriate confidentiality of their individual client.

2. The organization develops its own coaching and mentoring capacity

Organizations that develop their own internal coaching community can use a similar feedback process to the one used for external coaches. This allows direct comparison between the internal and external coaches, as well as ensuring that there is a standard method for looking at coaching benefits across different coaching providers. It is important that the feedback process includes some questions on the coaching service.

As described in Chapter 5, on organizing an internal coaching service and community, this feedback can be turned into an annual audit of the coaching service, which includes:

- number of clients seen and breakdown of different levels and functions;
- average length of contract;
- number of active coaches and average number of clients seen;
- average feedback ratings from clients on the value of the coaching, the coaching relationship, and the coaching service;
- scoring on initial goals achieved by client, coach, and client's manager;
- number of clients receiving coaching who improved their performance scores and achieved promotion, compared staff at the same level who did not receive coaching.

For this last area, the coaching service needs to be able to link its own feedback data to performance and promotion data in the wider organization. Many organizations are not ready to do this until they get to Step 5 in the coaching culture journey (see below). Other organizations engaged outside bodies to carry out an external audit of their coaching and the impact it has had. NHSI had an evaluation carried out by the Institute for Employment Studies. The Irish Electricity Supply Board used an HR consultancy and had an evaluation carried out by Dr. Brigid Milner, whose finding was that managers who had been coached reported very high levels of satisfaction and a high percentage reported that it had significantly shifted their work performance:

- 70.9 per cent said that it had supported the achievement of their work-related objectives.
- 71.8 per cent reported that it had improved the focus they have in their work role.
- 70.9 per cent stated that they approached their work role differently.

These are encouraging signs, but this remains the manager's own perception and only later in the evaluation process are companies ready to look at a shift in the perception of the manager by others through 360-degree feedback and hard measures of a positive shift in outcomes.

3. The organization and it leadership actively support coaching endeavours

At this stage, the organization starts to look at shifting its leadership culture and coaching being allied to this endeavour. This involves the organization having a clear sense of the change in leadership it requires and methods for evaluating where it is on the journey to achieving this.

Often at this stage, the organization will organize development days for their coaches. Some organizations provide these days for their external coaches and internal coaches separately, whereas others have combined events. These development sessions can be structured by:

- sharing the collective data with the coaches from the coaching audit;
- involving the coaches in a collaborative inquiry into the data;
- collectively exploring how the coaching service and the coaches can provide a more effective coaching provision; and then
- providing a learning input that addresses some of the emerging issues.

The organization at this stage may also institute regular reviews of all the external and individual coaches, to help them understand and process all the feedback they have received, explore what needs to change in their coaching, and what additional understanding, learning or development may help support this change.

4. Developing team coaching and engaging staff differently

At this stage, a variety of coaching processes might be in operation in various parts of the organization and therefore there needs to be different but comparable feedback mechanisms for each of them. Some organizations will have introduced team coaching, and in *Leadership Team Coaching* (Hawkins, 2011a) I provide a number of ways of evaluating team performance, both before and after team coaching. These methods involve both self-ratings by the team members, as well as 360-degree feedback from all the team's stakeholders, both within and outside the organization. I also argue for senior teams to have collective 'balanced scorecards' and key performance indicators, so the scores on the team coaching can be compared with the performance achievement of the team, as well as internal and external perceptions.

It is important at this stage to focus coaching more on the organization's strategic objectives. In their coaching strategy, the UK Foreign and Commonwealth Office wrote:

> Any coaching which benefits the individual performance will benefit the organization. But we get a more direct benefit if we pick priority strategic goals and use coaching techniques around them to push forward or consolidate progress.

They then proposed to their steering group a number of different items from the organization's strategic plan, where coaching could make a significant difference, and asked them to make some strategic choices about where coaching should be focused and the measurable difference it would want coaching to make. These included:

(a) coaching for groups who are underrepresented in the department to support the department's diversity agenda;
(b) individual and team coaching being linked to large change and transformation projects and evaluate the increase in the effectiveness of these projects;
(c) new entrants being given mentoring from those who have been in role a few years to increase early stage retention of good staff;
(d) identifying with directors and the board priority areas for the further use of targeted group, team or individual coaching.

At the same time, they suggested moving to an allocation of executive coaching through individuals making business cases for receiving internal or external coaching and limited resources being allocated against the quality of the business case. This illustrates how exploring how to evaluate the benefit of coaching can feed back into developing the coaching strategy and improving the targeting of coaching so that it has the greatest business benefit.

5. Coaching becomes embedded in the HR and performance management processes of the organization

At this stage, evaluation should be creating the links between coaching outputs and outcomes, by evaluating performance of those receiving coaching before and after coaching assignments. The HR department should be linking what is happening in the coaching service and coaching culture to other key people-measures in the organization. These should include:

- staff satisfaction survey results;
- staff retention figures. Just measuring the overall percentage of staff that leave per year is necessary but not sufficient. It is more important to measure the retention rate of the high-performing and high-potential staff. Who leaves the company is most critical, not just how many;
- the number of senior vacancies the company is able to fill through good internal candidates. Once again the number of senior vacancies filled from internal candidates can be misleading. An organization may well want to bring in some requisite diversity through external appointments. What is important is that the leadership strategy sets targets for internal and external appointments and can track whether they are meeting these through an effective talent pipeline supported by coaching;
- staff absenteeism figures. Some HR people strategies have established targets for reducing absenteeism, either to the average, by sector or geography, or to the 'best in class' in these areas;
- the number of staff grievances, disciplinary hearings and industrial tribunals – which should decrease as the coaching culture starts to take hold – and performance issues are tackled earlier and more appropriately.

The case study of Southern Railways in Chapter 9 provides a good example of linking coaching to achieving good results in these areas of evaluation. Also, the European Commission case study in Chapter 6 noted an increase in women managers, from 4 per cent in 1995 to 21.4 per cent in 2009, and a doubling at middle management level from 10.7 to 23.2 per cent.

6. Coaching becomes the predominant style of managing throughout the organization

Having established the links between coaching and individual performance improvement in the previous stage, the organization can move on to establish the link between coaching and the development of the leadership culture, the management culture, and the organizational culture and climate. Most organizations now carry out staff satisfaction surveys that include feedback on how employees view:

- the leadership of the organization;
- those who directly manage them;
- the climate of the organization; and
- the organizational culture.

Here again it is important that the questions are geared to measure not how popular the leaders or local managers are, but to whether the leadership and management can deliver the organizational goals. Thus questions on the leadership that ask employees to respond to the following statements on a 5-point scale (strongly disagree, disagree, neither disagree nor agree, agree, strongly agree) are more useful:

- The leadership of the organization has made the strategy of the organization clear and convincing.
- The leadership of the organization gives consistent and aligned messages.
- The leadership engages fully with all staff.
- The leadership listens to staff feedback and responds.

Also useful are statements on employees' direct managers, rated on the same scale, such as:

- My manager sets clear goals and objectives for the team.
- My manager sets clear goals and objectives for me.
- My manager has made a difference to my ability to meet my objectives.
- My manager has held helpful reviews of my performance.

7. Coaching becomes 'how we do business' with all our stakeholders and is linked to our value creation mission

So far, the evaluation processes have all focused internally, although they have moved from focusing on inputs to focusing on performance outputs, and from individual performance to team and organizational performance. In this final stage, it is now important to link the changes inside the organization with performance externally. Many organizations have a plethora of external feedback data but fail to integrate the different sets of data.

I have often asked senior executives the question:

How do you connect the data you get from multiple stakeholder sources: your customer feedback; your staff attitude survey; your press analysis; regulator and company analysts' reports; and investor feedback?

To date, I have never had a completely satisfactory answer, but nearly all the senior executives whom I have asked found it an important question. One chief executive replied: 'If we could integrate all that feedback, we would have a powerful aerial view, which would transform our ability to steer our organization!' Unfortunately in most organizations, the sales department manages the customer feedback, the marketing department manages the press analysis, the human relations department manages the staff attitude survey, corporate affairs manage the investor feedback, and the financial director manages the analysts' and regulatory reports.

Multiple stakeholder perceptions, when they are joined up, provide a valuable intermediate measure of change in organizational performance and value creation. To overcome this void between the short-term behavioural measures and long-term outcome measures – such as financial performance, analysts' ratings, customer and staff retention and attraction, and similar measures – we have developed several organizational 360-degree feedback assessment tools. One of these, 'descriptor analysis', enables the organization to view how it is perceived by all its key stakeholders, and how the stakeholders would like to perceive the organization (see Hawkins and Smith, 2006; Hawkins, 2011a).

Coaching and the debate on 'return on investment'

In recent years, there has been an upsurge of interest in 'return on investment' for all types of coaching expenditure. This can be seen in the number of conference sessions, articles, and academic papers, as well as the number of coaching strategies that are now including the phrase 'return on investment' in their coaching strategy. Some of this upsurge is driven by the concerns, or possibly anxiety, of coaches and coaching managers who have to defend their expenditure, in times of austerity and financial scrutiny of all budget overhead items. Thus, in the Foreign and Commonwealth Office strategy quoted in Chapter 3, they wrote:

Coaching is an investment, not a budget item.

At other times, this upsurge is driven by the challenge from the senior executives to all parts of the business, not only to reduce costs through greater efficiency, but to become more effective by challenging how each part of the organization can deliver greater value. Thus in the Irish Supply Board case study in Chapter 7, we see the coaching community addressing the question:

> How we can double the value from coaching in our organization?

There has also been a strong reaction to this focus, which has taken different forms. Some have argued that the results are too difficult to measure, as you can never separate out the impact of coaching from other developmental inputs that have also been involved, or from contextual changes that will have affected performance outcomes. When studying changes in individuals or groups of people, within complex and ever-changing systemic contexts, striving for empirically based scientific objectivity will always be as useful as looking for gold at the end of the rainbow! However, that does not mean that the quest for more effective and rigorous evaluation is in itself foolish, but rather we should be using a more appropriate research paradigm and appropriate research validity measures. In the last thirty years, there has been much progress in developing research methodology that is more appropriate than strict scientific empiricism, which requires laboratory conditions, removal of other influences, fixed contexts, and control groups. For studying human change in complex and changing systemic contexts, research methodology such as action research (Reason, 1988, 1994; Reason and Bradbury, 2000) is more suitable as it has a more phenomenological process with its own appropriate validity criteria. In the case of coaching culture, this includes procedures that involve:

- more rigorous data collection;
- multiple, albeit subjective, sources that can be cross-referenced;
- data being collected in similar ways at repeated intervals;
- conflicts of interest being named and managed;
- comparisons between different groups within the organization with different developmental provision;
- comparisons with data collected in other similar organizations.

The research would never deliver proof of linear cause and effect between coaching and performance outcome. That will always be impossible, as people and organizations do not function by linear cause and effect. What it will deliver is patterns indicative of the sort of coaching that creates the best results, how best to organize coaching, where to focus it for the best return on investment, and so on.

Writers such as Sherman and Freas argue that the shift in the culture will be obvious and clearly of value:

> When you create a culture of coaching, the result may not be directly measurable in dollars. But we have yet to find a company that can't

> benefit from more candour, less denial, richer communications, conscious development of talent, and disciplined leaders who show compassion for people.
>
> (Sherman and Freas, 2004: 90)

Others, of course, will argue that moral goodness is not enough of a foundation to sustain such an important enterprise. So a small but increasing number of organizations have begun to put in place some measurement of return on investment on their coaching expenditure.

Return on investment is traditionally defined as the amount of profit, before tax and after depreciation from an investment made, usually expressed as a percentage of the original total cost invested. A number of writers have used this outcome variable in their studies of coaching and claimed return on investment of between 600 and 700 per cent (Anderson, 2001; McGovern et al., 2001; Parker-Wilkins, 2006).

The 2010 Executive Coaching Survey, by Sherpa Executive Coaching in Texas, obtained returns from over 200 HR professionals from a wide variety of companies. Of these, 87 per cent saw the value of executive coaching as either 'somewhat high' or 'very high'. However, only 18 per cent of the HR professionals calculated the return on investment on their coaching expenditure, although this was up from 7 per cent on the previous year's survey, substantially more than a twofold increase.

A relatively simple way of calculating return on investment following the Sherpa methodology is laid out below.

- For every coaching contract, collect the issues addressed by the coaching and, for each, estimate the cost of not addressing that issue, or the costed benefit of a performance improvement (e.g. rise in productivity of the team £24,000 + reduction in staff turnover £36,000 = total benefit £60,000).
- Multiply by the percentage attributed by the individual coachee or team to the coaching (e.g. the coachee reports that 50 per cent of the productivity was directly attributable to the coaching and 20 per cent of the reduced staff turnover). This gives us figures of £12,000 and £7200 = £19,200 for the coaching benefit. More sophisticated measurement would be achieved by asking the coachee's boss and subordinates also to estimate this percentage and average the figures out.
- Multiply by the degree of confidence in the estimation, say 80 per cent = £15,360 adjusted coaching benefit.
- Subtract the total cost of the coaching = £5000, which gives a net benefit of £10,360.
- Then, to calculate the return on investment we divide the net benefit £10,360 by the coaching cost £5000 = 207.2 per cent.

This is clearly not an inexact science, with a great deal of subjective judgement. However, we are likely to see increasing pressure to measure the return on investment in coaching over the coming years and hence a development in the sophistication of such measurement. To evaluate the coaching culture as opposed to individual coaching assignments involves more rigorous measurement that looks at the impact of coaching right along the organization's relational value chain (see Chapter 11). Organizations need to be supported by the development of quality research processes from the academic wing of the coaching profession, but this too, as I will show below, is still in the early stages of development.

Coaching research

In their review of research on coaching, De Meuse et al. (2009: 117) write:

> While executive coaching is gaining popularity, the professional application of coaching, our understanding of when to use coaching and the evaluation of its effectiveness has lagged far behind.

They continue: 'In academia, review studies consistently have concluded that there is a paucity of empirical data to support the anecdotal evidence that coaching produces positive outcomes' and they reference Feldman and Lankau (2005), Kampa-Kokesch and Anderson (2001), and Mackie (2007).

De Meuse et al. (2009) then undertook a meta-analysis of the coaching research they could locate. Although there has been a marked upsurge in papers on coaching in scholarly journals, with English (2006) reporting a 300 per cent increase in the number of such papers between 1994–1999 and 2000–2004, the number of research studies is relatively small. Most research has been based on retrospective studies, where perceptions of the coaching and progress made were collected mostly from the coaches. De Meuse and colleagues could only find a very small sample of statistical studies of executive coaching carried out by external coaches that used pre- and post-coaching ratings, and only a few of these collected data from sources other than the coachee. (These also asked the coachee's line manager and/or the coach.) Unsurprisingly, where multiple perspectives were collected, the coachees rated their improvement through coaching higher than was rated by others. However, for the six studies that met their very strict criteria, De Meuse et al. concluded: 'executive coaching generally leads to a moderate-to-large amount of improvement in the coachee's skill and/or performance ratings' (p. 121).

De Meuse et al. (2009) also surveyed ten retrospective research studies and applied three of the four levels of Kirkpatrick's (1977) widely used model of evaluating training interventions: (a) reactions to coaching, (b) coaching effectiveness (as assessed through change or improvement in skills or performance at the individual level), and (c) coaching impact at the organizational level. Across the studies surveyed, 75–95 per cent of participants had favourable ratings of their coaching and nearly all studies indicated that the participants' individual effectiveness had improved. One of the most interesting studies is that of Parker-Wilkins (2006), whose respondents stated that coaching had assisted them on three main competencies: (i) leadership behaviours, 82 per cent; (ii) building teams, 41 per cent; and (iii) developing staff, 36 per cent. Only a small number of studies reviewed looked at the coaching impact at the organizational level. They all reported positive benefits but looked at different impacts: Talboom (1999) looked at the impact of coaching on subordinate absence rates; Anderson (2001), the impact of coaching on productivity and employee satisfaction; and Landale (2005), the impact on leadership, management teams, and business deliverables. Interestingly in this last study, twice as many respondents (67 per cent) reported an improvement in their personal life–work balance as reported an improvement in business deliverables (33 per cent).

In their review of research, De Meuse et al. (2009) concluded that, although there is a great deal of evidence that coaching does produce improvements in individual effectiveness, there is less evidence that it positively impacts on organizational improvement. There is an urgent need for more rigorous, consistent, and multi-faceted research that looks at the three levels of the Kirkpatrick scale mentioned above.

One of the challenges for coaching research is to show how personal development of the coachee translates into behaviour change and how this impacts business performance and value creation. To this end, Leedham (2005) proposed a pyramid model of research on executive coaching in organizations that shows the connections between coaching inputs at the bottom level, linking to inner personal benefits, to outer personal benefits, and from there to business results (see Figure 13.1).

In this book, I have argued that the emphasis on individual coaching as the only route to creating business results, is too limiting. We need to increase the amount of team coaching that leads to better team performance, so as to create a coaching environment that directly develops the overall organizational culture, business performance, and shared value in the wider stakeholder community. So building on Leedham (2005), I have constructed a new model of coaching research (see Figure 13.2).

In addition to Leedham's and De Meuse and colleagues' arguments for more rigorous research on coaching outcomes, I would advocate that more extensive research needs to be carried out on:

- how a coaching culture can develop a coach's skills and attributes as well as coaching processes, and reciprocally be developed by them;

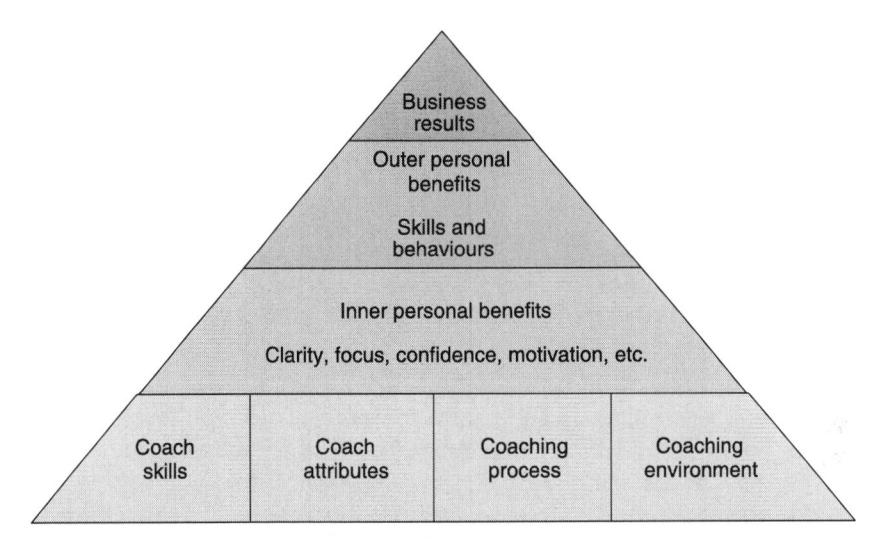

EVALUATION, RESEARCH, AND RETURN ON INVESTMENT **173**

Figure 13.1 Leedham's (2005) model of coaching research.

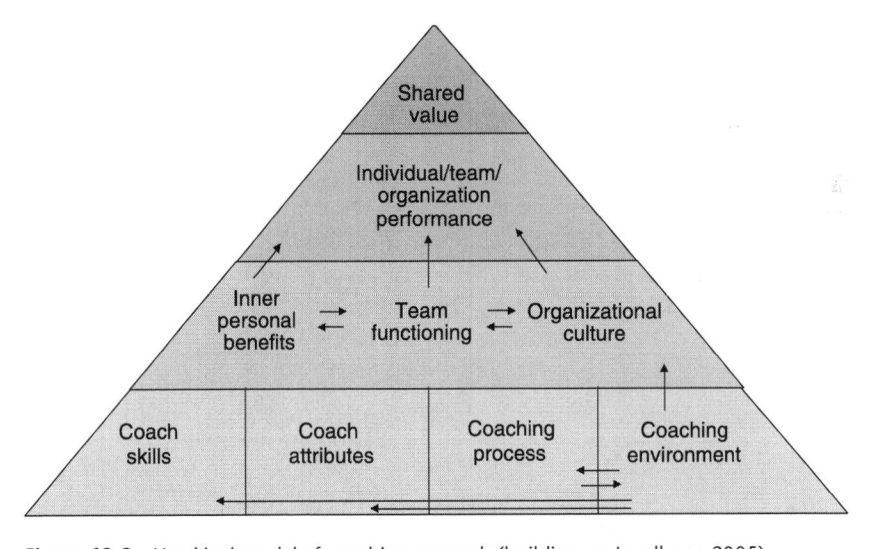

Figure 13.2 Hawkins' model of coaching research (building on Leedham, 2005).

- how a coaching culture can develop the organizational culture in the required direction;
- how team coaching can improve team performance and thus business results, and how it impacts the organizational culture;
- how personal coaching impacts on team performance;

- how individual, team, and organizational performance impact on the creation of shared value across the wider stakeholder community.

Conclusion

At each stage of developing a coaching culture, it is important that the organization establishes:

- clear standards for all aspects of the coaching inputs;
- clear objectives for the outputs expected at the individual, team, and organizational levels;
- how the individual and team benefits from coaching translate into improved organizational performance, culture change, and the fulfilment of strategic objectives;
- how the strategy objectives, organizational culture, and performance improvement create shared value in the wider stakeholder community;
- methods of evaluation for each of the above.

Some organizations will have the capacity to do this internally, others will seek the assistance of external consultants and/or researchers, both to help establish the linked processes and to carry out a coaching audit.

Such coaching audits and evaluation can then deliver clear information and knowledge to help the organization develop and focus its coaching processes and interventions. In addition, such audits provide the foundation for wider research across organizations into the most effective ways of coaching and developing a coaching culture. For coaching in organizations to embrace the next phase of its development, there needs to be much greater dialogue between senior executives, coaching managers, coaching providers, and researchers in the field. There is an urgent need to develop some more shared language and frameworks within which to have such dialogue.

14 Conclusion: the challenges going forward

The author Tom McCarthy, on the BBC Four programme 'Birth of the Novel' (15 February 2011), said that every novel ought to contain within it, its own negation, an embedded anti-novel, which like the grit in the oyster, creates a pearl of lasting quality. So before ending this book and this thesis on ways of creating a coaching culture, let me take a little while to share the antithesis – the reasons that should make you beware of those advocating a coaching culture. Many of us have been around organizational development for enough time to see many innovations and new development processes become 'flavours of the year' and quickly come and go. Each is born on a wave of enthusiasm and each ends beached up on the sands of disappointed expectations.

Some of these processes become an imagined holy grail, an abstracted notion that is seen as an end in itself, while forgetting that at best it can only be a means to serve a greater end than its own success. Other initiatives survive but lose their radical and innovatory life-blood by becoming an HR edifice, over-bureaucratized and self-serving. The developmental endeavour becomes constrained by being over-measured and tied up in too many complex bureaucratic processes. The supporting machinery takes more time and effort than the central activity. It has been said to me that a coaching culture is a mere chimera and one pessimist described it to me as a fantasy image of an oasis in the desert sands of organizational existence. One senior executive suggested that a coaching culture was just a new name for good management and relating well to people.

Another danger of a book such as this is that it over-complicates the journey and the processes needed and suggests that everything can be planned and created using a rational step-by-step approach. I began the book with a short maxim:

> To plant a tree is to leave a legacy. To create a garden is to change the ecology. Yet the garden must always leave space for wilderness to work its own magic.

To truly create a coaching culture is to change the ecology of an organization, the way it relates and connects internally and externally. However, as the maxim suggests, this cannot be done just by rational planning or by following somebody else's recipe. I hope there is much you can learn from the many models and examples in this book, but in the end each organization has to create its own journey and leave space for grace and for wilderness, where unexpected emergent change can surprise, delight, and at times confound the best laid plans.

So, if we deconstruct the notion of the coaching culture from the complex models and steps I have so far outlined, what do we find? All initiatives to create a coaching culture are attempts to take a mixture of coaching-related ingredients and bring them together in an integrated way that is more than the sum of the parts, to effect a shift in the organizational culture that creates real shared value for the organization and all its key stakeholders. These ingredients include:

- formal coaching by internal and/or external trained coaches;
- coaching supervision;
- the use of coaching skills for managing performance and development;
- a coaching style of managing, leading, and engaging staff and stakeholders;
- a coaching approach to developing teams (both leadership teams and project teams, virtual and co-located).

To sustain these ingredients and help them to connect and align in the most valuable way requires:

- sponsorship from leadership at the top of the organization, combined with innovation and joined up activity from people in the middle of the organization;
- alignment with all other important initiatives in the organization as well as its mission, strategy, and objectives;
- supporting mechanisms in selection, performance management, talent management, and promotion and reward.

If we deconstruct this further we might argue that a coaching culture is one aspect of creating a learning culture and a learning culture is just one aspect of creating a highly engaged, constantly renewing and innovating, high-performing culture. Even this is not an end in itself, but is in service of creating shared value (Porter and Kramer, 2011) throughout the organization, its stakeholders, and wider system.

If we go even further in our deconstruction, we need to ask: 'What is the essence of coaching, once we strip away all the theories and models, the different schools and methodologies, and the mushrooming multi-billion dollar business?' At its heart, coaching provides some skills and disciplines to aid generative conversations. These are conversations that generate new thinking, previously unknown to either party, which arises out of the quality of the relationship. Conversations are not, in the words of the scientist David Bohm (1987, 1996), about exchanging pre-cooked thoughts, but thinking afresh together. Bohm, like a number of other influential writers (Grudin, 1996; Zeldin, 1998; Issacs, 1999; Wheatley, 2002; Senge et al., 2005), has shown how dialogue and generative conversations are at the heart of shifting thinking, mindsets, assumptions and emotions, and are thus the life blood of organizational transformation and renewal.

Dialogue is a style of communicating that both enhances learning for all involved and ensures that necessary information is shared, decision making and planning are a joint activity, and development is collaboratively owned and managed. Bohm wrote that dialogue is:

> based on the Greek 'dia' meaning 'through' and 'logos' meaning 'the word'. But what is signified here is not the word as such (i.e. the sound) but its meaning. *Dialogue is a free flow of meaning between people.* We may use here the image of a stream flowing between two banks.
>
> What is essential for dialogue is that while a person may prefer a certain position, a person does not hold to it non-negotiably. Such a person is ready to listen to others with sufficient sympathy and interest to understand the meaning of the other's position properly and is ready to change his or her own point of view if there is good reason to do so.
>
> . . . it will happen when people are able to face their disagreements without either confrontation or polite avoidance of the issue, and when they are willing to explore together points of view to which they may not personally subscribe.
>
> (Bohm, 1989: 61 emphasis added)

Bill Issacs (1999) defines dialogue as 'a conversation with a center, not sides'. He continues:

> It is a way of taking the energy of our differences and channelling it toward something that has never been created before. It lifts us out of polarization and into a greater common sense, and is thereby a means for accessing the intelligence and coordinated power of groups of people.
>
> (Issacs, 1999: 19)

In my own writing and teaching, I contrast dialogue with debate, discussion, and negotiation, and show how dialogue can be thought of as meaning that flows between two or more people. Here the emphasis is on trying to understand the experience and reality of the other by imaginatively 'seeing through their eyes' or 'walking in their shoes'. In an effective dialogue there is a search for new meaning that can transform perspectives, create new insights, and develop new and more effective action.

One of the most important contributions that coaching has brought to the workplace has been to increase the quality of the conversations and help to move from debate, discussion, and information exchange to 'generative dialogue'. At the heart of creating a coaching culture is radically transforming the quality of our day-to-day conversations, whether in team meetings, by telephone, in the corridor or in more structured formal coaching sessions.

The scientific and industrial revolution stretched from the invention of the printing press in the late fifteenth century, through the inventions of machinery and steam power in the eighteenth and nineteenth centuries, to the petrol-driven transport and production of the twentieth century. It was built on ways of thinking that were fundamentally analytic and linear cause-and-effect problem solving. As we moved into the twenty-first century, much of this thinking has been taken over by the huge advances in computer capability while, at the same time, the learning at the edge of human advancement has changed significantly. The major challenges in organizations, between organizations, and in the world in general, require a different form of thinking that is connective, relational, holistic, and systemic. By its very nature, this thinking cannot be done solely by individuals cogitating alone (for individuals will, by definition, always have a limited perspective on any system of which they are a part), but by the ability of groups of people to think together.

Organizations are transformed by conversations, and it is the quality of these conversations that will determine the ability of any organization to renew itself and evolve in relation to its ever-changing environment. Coaches can be at the centre of the process of organizational transformation, by engendering better conversations and dialogue throughout the organization, both internally and in how stakeholders are engaged. In formal coaching sessions, the habits of inquiry and generative conversations can be developed in both parties. For this to happen there needs to be genuine dialogue in which the coach is also constantly learning and developing.

Coaches can also become the organizational 'reflectors' that help those swimming in the culture of the organization to step back and recognize what they have taken for granted, or become wilfully blind to. In her book *Wilful Blindness: How We Ignore the Obvious at Our Peril*, Margaret Heffernan (2011) illustrates how we often stop noticing and stop speaking about the important patterns in our organizations, which, if unaddressed, will be destructive to its very existence. She shows how, at BP, Enron, and Lehman Brothers, many employees were aware of what was fundamentally going wrong, but the conversations to address the critical issues were not taking place. Better conversations are central to our very survival.

However, for real and sustained change, coaching cannot stop at developing better conversations between individuals, in teams, and between organizations and their stakeholders. Early in this book, I showed how coaching, if it only produces insight, increased awareness, and good intention, is stopping short of delivering full value. Coaching needs to build on generative dialogue to create generative action and move from better understanding of each other to partnering one another to achieve the change that can only come from joint action.

To create and sustain a coaching culture, it is necessary to provide coaching activity in all parts of the system, and to constantly attend to the quality and depth of the coaching in producing more effective leaders, managers, employees, teams, and stakeholder partnerships, which will create real shared value.

Coaching at a crossroads

In Chapter 1, I argued that coaching was at a crossroads. The exponential growth and spread of the field has given coaching a prominence that has led to more difficult questions being asked about the value it creates (Hawkins, 2008). Given the global economic downturn between 2008 and 2010 (excluding China, India, Brazil, and one or two other smaller countries), most organizations have been focusing on creating stringent reductions in all overhead costs, not only in the public sector but also in the commercial sector. Unless coaching is seen as an investment that delivers a real return in value, it will be one of the many non-essentials that will see savage cuts.

Coaching research has shown that coaching clearly delivers value to the individual coachee in terms of increased awareness, insight, skills, and focus. There is some evidence how the increased awareness and good intentions translate into improved executive performance, but much less how it translates into organizational and team learning, development, and transformation.

In looking at the future of coaching, I see three possible scenarios.

Scenario 1: plateau and decline

In this scenario, coaching fails to demonstrate its value beyond individual development and is seen by many senior executives as a luxury that can be cut in times of austerity. The public sector will continue to cut all external coaching and put further pressure on internal coaches to make their services spread further, in a shorter time, without the requisite support infrastructure.

Partially established coaching infrastructures are dismantled and many internal coaches leave to try and set up externally but struggle to find work. What does remain is an increasing expectation that all managers have some basic coaching skills and ability in how they lead, manage, and develop their own people.

Scenario 2: a benefit for the privileged

This scenario also envisions severe cuts to coaching expenditure but the coaching that remains becoming highly targeted on senior leaders and hand-picked future talent that is being fast-tracked. Some coaching will still be attached to leadership development programmes. There will be a greater divide between the richer companies who can still afford coaching and smaller, lesser profitable companies and the public sector and civil society, who will have to cut non-essentials. In this scenario, there will be continued growth of coaching in fast-growing economies such as China, India, and Brazil.

Scenario 3: coaching finds a new phase of development

In this scenario, coaching enters a new but different phase of growth. The coaching profession and business coaches fully embrace the need to deliver personal and organizational benefit. More research shows the link between coaching, coaching cultures, organizational performance and value creation. Coaching becomes more strongly linked not only to manager and leader development, but leadership and organizational development. Senior leaders recognize that coaching is an essential aspect of building organizational agility, resilience, renewal, and transformation. Coaching becomes a key part of all organizational change endeavours.

For Scenario 3 to emerge requires coaches, coach trainers, coaching organizations, internal coaching communities, coach organizers, and buyers to embrace five critical and interconnecting challenges:

1. The need for all individual coaching in companies to focus not just on personal awareness, insight, and good intentions, but on outcome objectives that improve individual, team, and organizational performance and deliver value to the stakeholders. This will involve highly effective three-way contracting, reviewing, and evaluating, as well as ways of supervising the individual–organizational double benefit through harvesting the organizational learning.

2. The need for a greater focus on systemic team coaching that supports the development of high-performing teams and effective collective leadership and moves way beyond team away-days that facilitate team bonding.

3. The need not only to integrate the work of external and internal coaches, but also to ensure that their work has the necessary sustaining mechanisms to build coaching into the fabric of the organization.

4. That there is a coaching strategy that integrates all the steps to building a coaching culture and embraces the culture change necessary for the organization to successfully transform and renew.

5. That a coaching style is adopted by each organization that can be used with internal leadership and management and for external engagement with stakeholders. It can thus create the integration along the relational value chain from stakeholder experience right through to the leadership culture.

Only by grasping these five challenges will coaching in organizations start to make the next ascent of its own developmental journey and not plateau and atrophy, or become another benefit for the privileged few.

Where do coaching strategies and establishing coaching cultures go from here?

In my visits over the last two years to many enterprising and vibrant coaching cultures, I have been heartened by the commitment, the courage, and the determination of the coaching managers, the coaches, and the senior leaders to make a real difference to their organization, through developing their people. It has often been said that the phrase 'People are our greatest asset' is one of the great lies in organizational life, as it is preached but not enacted. However, in the organizations I have studied who are struggling to build a coaching culture, many of the leaders, managers, and employees were clearly walking this talk.

It was also encouraging to see how many of these early pioneers are networking closely together across organizations, and across sectors and countries, to learn from each other and quickly spread best practice. Most of this networking is informal, but some of the professional bodies are now supporting the informal processes, with facilitated exchange forums and collaborative conferences. My hope is that this book will support and extend this spread of best practice, for clearly no organization is, or can be, the exemplar or benchmark that can show others how it is done. A number of the companies cited in this book have brilliantly developed one, two or three pieces of the complete jigsaw puzzle from which others can learn. None of them has arrived at having all the elements of the coaching infrastructure in place. Only by continuing to work together can internal and external coaches, coach buyers and providers, academics, researchers, and practitioners assemble the whole picture of a good coaching strategy. Even with a complete coaching strategy and a well-assembled coaching infrastructure strongly linked to the business mission and strategy, we will still have much work to do, both in deepening and expanding the quality of the coaching and constantly evolving the wider organizational culture to best meet the fast changing needs of the external context.

Let us, then, set out on the journey to create better coaching strategies that will enable and sustain a more connected, effective, and agile culture in our organizations, as we encounter an ever-increasing volatility of change in the future.

Bibliography

Anderson, M.C. (2001) *Executive briefing: case study on the return on investment of Executive Coaching* (available at: http://www.metrixglobal.net; accessed 1 December 2011).

Anderson, V., Rayner, C. and Schyns, B. (2009) *Coaching at the Sharp End: The Role of the Line Managers in Coaching at Work*. London: Chartered Institute of People Development.

Argyris, C. (1993) *Knowledge in Action*. San Francisco, CA: Jossey-Bass.

Argyris, C. and Schön, D. (1978) *Organizational Learning*. Reading, MA: Addison-Wesley.

Attwood, M., Pedler, M., Pritchard, S. and Wilkinson, D. (2003) *Leading Change: A Guide to Whole Systems Working*. Bristol: Policy Press.

Bachkirova, T., Jackson, P. and Clutterbuck, D. (eds.) (2011) *Coaching and Mentoring Supervision: Theory and Practice*. Maidenhead: Open University Press.

Balint, M., Balint, E., Gosling, R. and Hildebrand, P. (1966) *A Study of Doctors*. London: Tavistock Publications.

Bateson, G. (1972) *Steps to an Ecology of Mind*. New York: Ballantine.

Beck, D. and Cowan, C. (1996) *Spiral Dynamics: Mastering Values, Leadership and Change*. Oxford: Blackwell Business.

Beckhard, R. and Harris, R. (1977) *Organizational Transitions: Managing Complex Change*. Reading, MA: Addison-Wesley.

Belbin, M. (2004) *Management Teams: Why they Succeed or Fail*. London: Heinemann.

Binney, G., Wilke, G. and Williams, C. (2005) *Living Leadership: A Practical Guide for Ordinary Heroes*. London: Prentice-Hall.

BlessingWhite (2008) *The Coaching Conundrum 2009: Building a Coaching Culture that Drives Organizational Success*. Princeton, NJ: BlessingWhite.

Bohm, D. (1987) *Unfolding Meaning* (edited by D. Factor). London: Routledge & Kegan Paul.

Bohm, D. (1989) Meaning and information, in P. Pylkkanen (ed.) *The Search for Meaning*. Wellingborough: Crucible/Thorsons.

Bohm, D. (1994) *Thought as System*. London: Routledge.

Bohm, D. (1996) *On Dialogue*. London: Routledge.

Boyatzis, R. and McKee, A. (2005) *Resonant Leadership: Renewing Yourself and Connecting to Others, through Mindfulness, Hope and Compassion*. Boston, MA: Harvard Business School Press.

Braddick, C. (2010) *More Process, Less Insight? Survey Report: Trends in Executive Coach Selection*. Braintree: Graham Braddick Partnership (available at: carolbraddick.com; accessed 1 December 2011).

Burke, W. (2002) *Organization Change: Theory and Practice*. London: Sage Publications.

CapGemini (2010) *Cutting Costs while Growing Customer Focus through BeLean®*. New York: CapGemini.

Caplan, J. (2003) *Coaching for the Future: How Smart Companies Use Coaching and Mentoring*. London: CIPD.

Carr, R. (2005) *Coaching Statistics, Facts, Guesses, Conventional Wisdom and the State of the Industry*. Victoria, BC: Peer Resources.

Carr, R. (2008) Coach referral services: do they work?, *International Journal of Evidence Based Coaching and Mentoring*, 6(2): 114–18.

Chartered Institute of Personnel and Development (CIPD) (2004) *Re-organising for Success: A Survey of HR's Role in Change*. London: CIPD (available at: http://www.cipd.co.uk/surveys; accessed 8 April 2011).

Chartered Institute of Personnel and Development (CIPD) (2008) *Learning and Development: Annual Survey Report*. London: CIPD (avaliable at: http://www.cipd.co.uk/subjects/lrnanddev/general/_lrngdevsvy.htm; accessed 8 April 2011).

Chartered Institute of Personnel and Development (CIPD) (2009) *Taking the Temperature of Coaching* (available at: http://www.cipd.co.uk/NR/rdonlyres/BC060DD1-EEA7-4929-9142-1AD7333F95E7/0/5215_Learning_talent_development_survey_report.pdf; accessed 8 April 2011).

Clark, M. (2002) The relationship between employees' perception of organizational climate and customer retention rates in a major UK retail bank, *Journal of Strategic Marketing*, 10: 93–113.

Clutterbuck, D. (2007) *Coaching the Team at Work*. London: Nicholas Brealey.

Clutterbuck, D. (2010) Team coaching, in E. Cox, T. Bachkirova and D. Clutterbuck (eds) *The Complete Handbook of Coaching*. London: Sage.

Clutterbuck, D. and Megginson, D. (2005) *Making Coaching Work: Creating a Coaching Culture*. London: CIPD.

Collins, J.C. (1999) Turning goals into results: the power of catalytic mechanisms, *Harvard Business Review*, July/August, pp. 71–82.

Collins, J.C. (2001) *Good To Great: Why Some Companies Make the Leap and Others Don't*. London: Random House.

Cooperrider, D.L. and Srivastva, S. (1987) Appreciative inquiry in organizational life, in R.W. Woodman and W.A. Passmore (eds) *Research in Organizational Change and Development*, Vol. 1. Greenwich, CT: JAI Press.

Corporate Leadership Council (2003) *Maximizing Returns on Professional Executive Coaching*. Washington, DC: Corporate Executive Board.

Corporate Research Forum (2006) *Obtaining Value from Executive Coaching*. London: Corporate Research Forum.

Coutu, D. and Kauffman, C. (2009) What can coaches do for you?, *Harvard Business Review*, 87(1): 91–7.
De Hahn, E. (2008) *Relational Coaching: Journeys Towards Mastering One-To-One Learning*. Chichester: Wiley.
De Meuse, K.P., Dai, G. and Lee, R.J. (2009) Evaluating the effectiveness of executive coaching: beyond ROI?, *Coaching: An International Journal of Theory, Research and Practice*, 2(2): 117–34.
Dixon, N.M. (1998) *Dialogue at Work: Making Talk Developmental for People and Organizations*. London: Lemos & Crane.
Dyke, G. (2004) *Greg Dyke: Inside Story*. London: HarperCollins.
Eleftheriadou, Z. (1994) *Transcultural Counselling*. London: Central Book Publishing.
Ellinger, A.D. (2005) Contextual factors influencing learning in a workplace setting: the case of 'reinventing itself company', *Human Resource Development Quarterly*, 16(3): 389–415.
English, M. (2006) Business print media coverage of executive coaching: a content analysis. Doctoral dissertation, Capella University, Minneapolis, MN.
Feldman, D.C. and Lankau, M.J. (2005) Executive coaching: a review and agenda for future research, *Journal of Management*, 31(6): 829–48.
Fisher, R. and Ury, W. (1991) *Getting to Yes: Negotiating Agreement without Giving In*, 2nd edn. Harmondsworth: Penguin.
Frisch, M.H. (2001) The emerging role of the internal coach, *Consulting Psychology Journal*, 53(4): 240–50.
Garratt, B. (1987) *The Learning Organization*. London: Fontana/Collins.
Garratt, B. (1996) *The Fish Rots from the Head: The Crisis in our Boardrooms*. London: HarperCollins Business.
Garratt, B. (2003) *Thin on Top*. London: Nicholas Brealey.
George, W. (2003) *Authentic Leadership: Rediscovering the Secrets of Creating Lasting Value*. San Francisco, CA: Jossey-Bass.
Gerstner, L. (2002) *Who Says Elephants Can't Dance? How I Turned Around IBM*. London: HarperCollins.
Goleman, D. (1996) *Emotional Intelligence: Why it can Matter More than IQ*. New York: Bantam Books.
Goleman, D. (1998) *Working with Emotional Intelligence*. New York: Bantam Books.
Goleman, D. (2009) *Ecological Intelligence*. New York: Broadway Books.
Grant, A.M. and Cavanagh, M.J. (2004) Towards a profession of coaching: sixty-five years of progress and challenges for the future, *International Journal of Evidence Based Coaching and Mentoring*, 2(1): 1–16.
Grudin, R. (1996) *On Dialogue: An Essay in Free Thought*. Boston, MA: Houghton Mifflin.
Hackman, J.R. (2002) *Leading Teams: Setting the Stage for Great Performance*. Cambridge, MA: Harvard Business Books.

Hackman, J.R. and Wageman, R. (2005) A theory of team coaching, *Academy of Management Review*, 30(2): 269–87.

Hardingham, A., with Brearley, M., Moorhouse, A. and Venter, B. (2004) *The Coach's Coach: Personal Development for Personal Developers*. London: CIPD.

Hargrove, R. (2003) *Masterful Coaching*. San Francisco, CA: Jossey-Bass/Pfeiffer.

Hawkins, P. (1986) Living the learning. PhD thesis, University of Bath Management School, Bath.

Hawkins, P. (1991) The spiritual dimension of the learning organization, *Management Education and Development*, 22(3): 172–87.

Hawkins, P. (1993) *Shadow Consultancy*, Working Paper. Bath: Bath Consultancy Group.

Hawkins, P. (1994) The changing view of learning, in J. Burgoyne (ed.) *Towards the Learning Company*. London: McGraw-Hill.

Hawkins, P. (1997) Organizational culture: sailing between evangelism and complexity. *Human Relations*, 50(4): 417–40.

Hawkins, P. (1999) *Organizational Unlearning*. Keynote address at the Learning Company Conference, University of Warwick, Warwick.

Hawkins, P. (2005) *The Wise Fool's Guide to Leadership*. Winchester: O Books.

Hawkins, P. (2006) Coaching supervision, in J. Passmored (ed.) *Excellence in Coaching*. London: Kogan Page.

Hawkins, P. (2008) The coaching profession: key challenges, *Coaching: An International Journal of Theory, Research and Practice*, 1(1): 28–38.

Hawkins, P. (2009) Developing an effective coaching strategy, *Global Focus: The EFMD Business Magazine Supplement*, 3(3): 15–19.

Hawkins, P. (2010) Coaching supervision, in E. Cox, T. Bachkirova and D. Clutterbuck (eds) *The Complete Handbook of Coaching*. London: Sage.

Hawkins, P. (2011a) *Leadership Team Coaching: Developing Collective Transformational Leadership*. London: Kogan Page.

Hawkins, P. (2011b) Building emotional, ethical and cognitive capacities in coaches: a developmental model of supervision, in J. Passmore (ed.) *Supervision in Coaching*. London: Kogan Page.

Hawkins, P. (2011c) Systemic coaching supervision, in T. Bachkirova, P. Jackson and D. Clutterbuck (eds) *Coaching and Mentoring Supervision: Theory and Practice*. Maidenhead: Open University Press.

Hawkins, P. and Chesterman, D. (2006) *Every Teacher Matters*. London: Teacher Support Network.

Hawkins, P. and Schwenk, G. (2006) *Coaching Supervision*. London: CIPD Change Agenda.

Hawkins, P. and Schwenk, G. (2010) The interpersonal relationship in the training and supervision of coaches, in S. Palmer and A. McDowell (eds) *The Coaching Relationship: Putting People First*. London: Routledge.

Hawkins, P. and Schwenk, G. (2011) The seven-eyed model of supervision, in T. Bachkirova, P. Jackson and D. Clutterbuck (eds) *Coaching and Mentoring Supervision: Theory and Practice*. Maidenhead: Open University Press.

Hawkins, P. and Shohet, R. (2006) *Supervision in the Helping Professions*, 3rd edn. Maidenhead: Open University Press.

Hawkins, P. and Smith N. (2006) *Coaching, Mentoring and Organizational Consultancy: Supervision and Development*. Maidenhead: Open University Press/McGraw-Hill.

Hawkins, P. and Smith, N. (2010) Transformational coaching, in E. Cox, T. Bachkirova and D. Clutterbuck (eds) *The Complete Handbook of Coaching*. London: Sage.

Hawkins, P. and Wright, A. (2009) Being the change you want to see: developing the leadership culture at Ernst and Young, *Strategic HR Review*, 8(4): 17–23.

Hedberg, B. (1981) How organizations learn and unlearn, in P. Nystrom and W. Starbuck (eds) *Handbook of Organizational Design, Vol. 1: Adapting Organizations to Their Environments*. Oxford: Oxford University Press.

Heffernan, M. (2011) *Wilful Blindness: How We Ignore the Obvious at Our Peril*. London: Simon & Schuster.

Helminski, K. (1999) *The Knowing Heart*. Boston, MA: Shambhala.

Hersey, P. and Blanchard, K.H. (1977) *Management of Organizational Behavior Utilizing Human Resources*, 3rd edn. Englewood Cliffs, NJ: Prentice-Hall.

Hirschorn, L. and Gilmore, T. (1992) The new boundaries of the boundaryless company, *Harvard Business Review*, May/June, pp. 104–15.

Holbeche, L. (2005) *The High Performance Organization*. Oxford: Elsevier Butterworth-Heinemann.

Honey, P. and Mumford, A. (1982) *The Manual of Learning Styles*. Maidenhead: Peter Honey Publications.

Hooper, R.A. and Potter, J.R. (2000) *Intelligent Leadership: Creating a Passion for Change*. London: Random House.

Huffington, C. (1998) The system in the room: the extent to which coaching can change the organization, in D. Campbell and C. Huffington (eds) *Organizations Connected: A Handbook of Systemic Consultation, Systemic Thinking and Practice: Work with Organizations*. London: Karnac Books.

Hunt, J.M. and Weintraub, J.R. (2006) *The Coaching Organization: A Strategy for Development*. London: Sage.

Hutchinson, S. and Purcell, J. (2003) *Bringing Policies to Life: The Vital Role of Front Line Managers*. London: CIPD.

Hutchinson, S. and Purcell, J. (2007) *Line Managers' Role in Reward, Learning and Development*. Research into Practice Report. London: CIPD.

Illich, I. (1997) *Disabling Professions*. London: Marion Boyars.

International Coaching Federation (2011) *Core competencies* (www.coachfederation.org/research.../icf.../core-competencies/; accessed 12 March 2011).
Issacs, W. (1999) *Dialogue: And the Art of Thinking Together*. New York: Currency.
Jarvis, J., Lane, D.A. and Fillery-Travis, A. (2006) *The Case for Coaching: Making Evidence Based Decisions*. London: CIPD.
Kampa-Kokesch, S. and Anderson, M.Z. (2001) Executive coaching: a comprehensive review of the literature, *Consulting Psychology Journal: Practice and Research*, 53: 205–28.
Kaplan, R.S. and Norton, D.P. (1992) The balanced scorecard – measures that drive performance. *Harvard Business Review*, January/February, pp. 71–9.
Kaplan, R.S. and Norton, D.P. (1996) *Translating Strategy into Action: The Balanced Scorecard*. Boston, MA: Harvard Business School Press.
Karpman, S. (1968) Fairy tales and script drama analysis (selected articles), *Transactional Analysis Bulletin*, 7(26): 39–43.
Katzenbach, J. and Smith, D. (1993a) The discipline of teams, *Harvard Business Review*, March/April, pp. 111–20.
Katzenbach, J. and Smith, D. (1993b) *The Wisdom of Teams: Creating the High-performance Organization*. Cambridge, MA: Harvard Business School Press.
Kempster, S. (2009) *How Managers Have Learnt to Lead*. Basingstoke: Palgrave Macmillan.
Kets de Vries, M.F.R. (2006) *The Leader on the Couch: A Clinical Approach to Changing People and Organizations*. San Francisco, CA: Jossey-Bass.
Kirkpatrick, D.L. (1977) Evaluating training programmes: evidence vs. proof, *Training and Development Journal*, 31(11): 9–12.
Kline, N. (1999) *Time to Think: Listening to Ignite the Human Mind*. London: Cassell.
Knights, A. and Poppleton, A. (2008) *Coaching in Organizations*. London: CIPD.
Kotter, J.P. (1995) Leading change: why transformation efforts fail, *Harvard Business Review*, March/April, pp. 59–67.
Landale, A. (2005) When coaching measures up, *Training Magazine*, October, p. 20.
Laske, O. (2003) Executive development as adult development, in J. Demick and C. Andreoletti (eds) *Handbook of Adult Development*. New York: Plenum/Kluwer.
Leedham, M. (2005) The coaching scorecard: a holistic approach to evaluating the benefits of business coaching, *International Journal of Evidence Based Coaching and Mentoring*, 3(2): 30–44.
Luthans, F. and Peterson, S.J. (2003) 360 degree feedback with systemic coaching: empirical analysis suggests a winning combination, *Human Resource Management*, 43: 243–56.

Mackie, D. (2007) Evaluating the effectiveness of executive coaching: where are we now and where do we need to be?, *Australian Psychologist*, 42: 310–18.

March, J.G. and Olsen, J.P. (1976) *Ambiguity and Choice in Organizations*. Bergen: Universitetsforlaget.

Marshall, J., Coleman, G. and Reason, P. (2011) *Leadership for Sustainability: An Action Research Approach*. Sheffield: Greenleaf.

Maxwell, A. (2011) Supervising the internal coach, in T. Bachkirova, P. Jackson and D. Clutterbuck (eds) *Coaching and Mentoring Supervision: Theory and Practice*. Maidenhead: Open University Press.

McDermott, M., Levenson, A. and Newton, S. (2007) What coaching can and cannot do for your organization, *Human Resource Planning*, 30(2): 30–7.

McGovern, J., Lindemann, M., Vergara, M., Murphy, S., Barker, L. and Warrenfeltz, R. (2001) Maximizing the impact of executive coaching: behavioral change, organizational outcomes and return on investment, *Manchester Review*, 6(1): 1–9.

McGurk, J. (2008) *Coaching and Buying Coaching Services Guide*. London: CIPD.

Megginson, D. and Clutterbuck, D. (2005) *Techniques for Coaching and Mentoring*. Oxford: Elsevier Butterworth-Heinemann.

Mintzberg, H. (1994) *The Rise and Fall of Strategic Planning: Reconceiving Roles for Planning, Plans and Planners*. New York: Simon & Schuster.

Obolensky, N. (2010) *Complex Adaptive Leadership: Embracing Paradox and Uncertainty*. Farnham: Gower.

O'Neill, M.B. (2000) *Executive Coaching with Backbone and Heart: A Systems Approach to Engaging Leaders with Their Challenges*. San Francisco, CA: Jossey-Bass.

Oshry, B. (1999) *Leading Systems: Lessons from the Power Lab*. San Francisco, CA: Berrett-Koehler.

Oshry, B. (2007) *Seeing Systems: Unlocking the Mysteries of Organizational Life*, 2nd edn. San Francisco, CA: Berrett-Koehler.

Ouchi, W.G. and Wilkins, L.G. (1985) Organizational culture, *Annual Review of Sociology*, 11: 457–83.

Pardey, D. (2011) *Mastery in Coaching: Integrity and Competence*. Presentation at the North East London University Conference, 7 March. London: Institute of Leadership and Management.

Parker-Wilkins, V. (2006) Business impact of executive coaching: demonstrating monetary value, *Industrial and Commercial Training*, 38: 122–7.

Passmore, J. (2010) *Supervision in Coaching*. London: Kogan Page.

Pedler, M. (1996) *Action Learning for Managers*. London: Lemos & Crane.

Pedler, M. (1997) What do we mean by action learning?, in M. Pedler (ed.) *Action Learning in Practice*. Aldershot: Gower.

Pedler, M., Burgoyne, J.G. and Boydell, T. (1991) *The Learning Company: A Strategy for Sustainable Development*. London: McGraw-Hill.

Pedler, M., Burgoyne, J.G. and Brook, C. (2005) What has action learning learnt to become, *Action Learning: Research and Practice*, 2(1): 49–68.

Peterson, D.B. (2010a) Good to great coaching: accelerating the journey, in G. Hernez-Broome and L.A. Boyce (eds) *Advancing Executive Coaching: Setting the Course for Successful Leadership Coaching*. San Francisco, CA: Jossey-Bass.

Peterson, D.B. (2010b) Executive coaching: a critical review and recommendations for advancing the practice, in S. Zedeck (ed.) *APA Handbook of Industrial and Organizational Psychology: Vol. 2. Selecting and Developing Members of the Organization*. Washington, DC: American Psychological Association.

Pettigrew, A. and McNulty, T. (1995) Power and influence in and around the boardroom, *Human Relations*, 48(8): 845–73.

Porter, M.E. and Kramer, M.R. (2011) Shared value: how to re-invent capitalism and unleash a wave of innovation and growth, *Harvard Business Review*, 89(1/2): 62–77.

Rackham, N. (1988) *SPIN Selling*. New York: McGraw-Hill.

Reason, P. (1988) *Human Inquiry in Action*. London: Sage.

Reason, P. (1994) *Participation in Human Inquiry*. London: Sage.

Reason, P. and Bradbury, H. (2000) *Handbook of Action Research: Participative Inquiry and Practice*. London: Sage.

Revans, R. (1998) *The ABC of Action Learning*. London: Lemos & Crane.

Rogers, C. (1967) *On Becoming a Person*. London: Constable.

RSA (1995) *Tomorrow's Company*. London: RSA.

Ryde, J. (2009) *Being White in the Helping Professions: Developing Effective Intercultural Awareness*. London: Jessica Kingsley.

Sadler, P. (2002) *Building Tomorrow's Company*. London: Kogan Page.

Scharma, C. O. (2007). *Theory U: Leading from the Future as it Emerges – The Social Technology of Presencing*. Cambridge: Society for Organizational Learning.

Schein, E.H. (1969) *Process Consultation: Its Role in Organizational Development*. London: Wesley.

Schein, E.H. (1985) *Organizational Culture and Leadership*. San Fransisco, CA: Jossey-Bass.

Schein, E.H. (2003) On dialogue, culture, and organizational learning, *Reflections*, 4(4): 27–38.

Senge, P. (1990) *The Fifth Discipline: The Art and Practice of the Learning Organization*. New York: Doubleday.

Senge, P. (2008) *The Necessary Revolution: How Individuals and Organizations are Working Together to Create a Sustainable World*. New York: Doubleday.

Senge, P., Kleiner, A., Ross, R., Roberts, C. and Smith, B. (1994) *The Fifth Discipline Fieldbook: Strategies and Tools for Building a Learning Organization*. New York: Doubleday.

Senge, P., Jaworski, J., Scharmer, C. and Flowers, B. (2005) *Presence: Exploring Profound Change in People, Organizations and Society*. New York: Doubleday.

Sherman, S. and Freas, A. (2004) The wild west of executive coaching, *Harvard Business Review*, 82(11): 82–90.

Stacey, R. (2010) *Complexity and Organizational Reality*. London: Routledge.

St. John-Brooks, K. (2010) What are the ethical challenges involved in being an internal coach?, *International Journal of Mentoring and Coaching*, VIII(1): 50–66.

Strumpf, C. (2002) Coaching from the inside: when, why and how?, in C. Fitzgerald and J. Garvey Berger (eds) *Executive Coaching: Practices and Perspectives*. Mountain View, CA: Davies Black Publishing.

Surowiecki, J. (2005) *The Wisdom of Crowds: Why the Many are Smarter than the Few*. London: Abacus.

Talboom, A.M. (1999) *The Welfare Sector Hits Hard: Exploratory Research after the Role of Coaching and Counselling within Organizations*. Nijmegen: Nijmegen Business School.

The Corporate Research Forum (2006) *Workshop: Managing Coaching in Organizations*. Berkhampstead: Ashridge Business School.

Thomson, P. and Graham, J. (2005) *A Woman's Place is in the Boardroom*. Basingstoke: Palgrave Macmillan.

Thomson, P. and Lloyd, T. (2011) *Women and the New Business Leadership*. Basingstoke: Palgrave Macmillan.

Thornton, C. (2010) *Group and Team Coaching*. Abingdon: Routledge.

Tichy, N. and Bennis, W. (2007) *Judgment: How Winning Leaders make Great Calls*. New York: Portfolio/Penguin.

Tichy, N. and Cohen, E. (2002) *The Leadership Engine: How Winning Companies Build Leaders at Every Level*. New York: HarperCollins.

Tichy, N. and McGill, A. (2003) *The Ethical Challenge: How to Lead with Unyielding Integrity*. San Francisco, CA: Jossey-Bass.

Torbert, W. (2004) *Action Inquiry: The Secret of Timely and Transforming Leadership*. San Francisco, CA: Berrett-Koehler.

Underhill, B.O., McAnally, K. and Koriath, J.J. (2007) *Executive Coaching for Results: The Definitive Guide to Developing Organizational Leaders*. San Francisco, CA: Berrett-Koehler.

Ury, W. (1992) *Getting Past No: Negotiating with Difficult People*. New York: Random House Business.

Van Ryn, M. and Heaney, C.A. (1997) Developing effective helping relationships in health eduction practice, *Health Education Behaviour*, 24: 683–702.

Wageman, R., Nunes, D.A., Burruss, J.A. and Hackman, J.R. (2008) *Senior Leadership Teams*. Cambridge, MA: Harvard Business School Press.

Walshyn, K.M. (2003) Executive coaching: an outcome study, *Consulting Psychology Journal: Practice and Research*, 55: 94–106.

Ward, G. (2008) Towards executive change: a psychodynamic group coaching model for short executive programs, *International Journal of Evidence Based Coaching and Mentoring*, 6(1): 67–78.

Welch, J. (2001) *Jack: What I have Learned Leading a Great Company and Great People*. New York: Warner Books.

Wheatley, M. (2002) *Turning to One Another: Conversations to Restore Hope to the Future*. San Francisco, CA: Berret-Keohler.

Whitmore, J. (2002) *Coaching for Performance: Growing People, Performance and Purpose*. London: Nicholas Brealey.

Witherspoon, R. and White, R.P. (1996) Executive coaching: a continuum of roles, *Consulting Psychology Journal: Practice and Research*, 48: 124–33.

Yip, G., Devinney, T. and Johnson, G. (2009) Measuring long term superior performance, *Long Range Planning*, 42(3): 390–413.

Zeldin, T. (1998) *Conversations: How Talk can Change Our Lives*. London: Harvill Press.

Zenger, J.H. and Stinnett, K. (2006) Leadership coaching: developing effective executives, *Chief Learning Officer*, 5(7): 44–7.

Index

360-degree feedback 55, 164–8
　assessment tool 168
　descriptor analysis 168
70:20:10 principle 14–15, 90
Academy of Executive Coaching 90
Accountability
　management of, 120
　to natural environment, 126
　social responsibility 126
Action learning 83–5
　definition of, 84
　protocols 84–5
　sets 85 157
Action planning 120
Action research 169
Active listening 118
Addictive behaviours 106
Analytical skills 73
Anderson, V., Rayner, C. and Schyns, B. 114–16, 120, 170
Annual review 101
APECS *see* Association for Professional Executive Coaching and Supervision
Appreciative inquiry 37–8
Appraisals *see* development conversations
Argyris and Schön 13, 53
Artefacts 22
Assessment centres 54
Association for Coaching 50
Association for Professional Executive Coaching and Supervision (APECS) 50, 65, 158
Audit *see* Evaluation

Bateson, Gregory 126–7
Bath Consultancy Group 87, 90, 155, 157
BBC *see* British Broadcasting Corporation
Behaviours 22, 160
Belbin, M. 55
Board
　development of, 39
　investor coaching and, 132–3
　role in commissioning 93

Boeing 129
Bohm, D. 177
Braddick, Carol 54
British Aerospace 91
British Airways 82, 127, 129
British Broadcasting Corporation (BBC) 47, 64–5, 68, 69, 106, 121, 157
　case study 72–8
BP 178
Building relationships 73
Burchell, Chris 122
Business Re-engineering 148
Business strategy 30, 41, 147–51

Cathay Pacific 129
Change agent 60
Change capability 105
Chartered Institute of Personnel and Development (CIPD) 11–12, 23, 53, 60, 169, 155
　Managing Change Agenda survey 69, 156–7
　definition of mentoring 62
　manager as coach, research on, 115
Chief executive 3–4, 56, 79
　training 72
CLEAR coaching model 91, 97–8, 133
　dialogue meeting 133
Clutterbuck, D. 92
Clutterbuck, D. and Megginson, D. 21, 100
Coach
　assessment of 74
　capabilities 50
　criteria 50–1
　external 76
　internal, assessment form 66
　interviews 53
　matching 55–7, 68–9
　mentor 74
　profile form 51–2
　selection 50–4
　supervisor, assignment of, 74
　training 67

Coaching
    action learning 83-4
    activity 142
    best practice 159, 181
    capabilities 50, 65, 74
    capacities 50, 65
    CLEAR model 91, 97-8, 117
    collective group 85
    communities, internal and external, 83
    competencies 50, 65, 73
    continuum model 115, 152-3
    contracting 117
    conversations, structure of, 117
    corridor 90-1
    culture 21-32
    culture map of, 30
    customers 127-9
    definition of, 41-2, 49
    development 103, 115, 153, 164-5
    developmental 60
    differences between mentoring and, 63
    effectiveness of, 152-9
    evaluation of, 71, 76-7, 143, 158, 160-8, 174
    four levels of engagement 118-19
    framework 116-17
    group 84-86
    GROW, model of, 117
    health 131-2
    infrastructure 26-7, 147-51, 181-2
    inquiry skills 120
    internal community, stages in forming, building and maintaining 64-71
    investor 132-3
    leadership 80-3
    manager development, 123
    matching process 55-7
    mentoring and, difference between, 62-3
    outcomes 28, 41, 48, 97, 160-1, 166
    outputs 28, 160-1, 166
    panel 47-59
    patient 131-2
    performance 152
    policy 49, 67
    pool 55-6
    practicum group 86, 157
    proactive 23
    quality of, 142-3
    reflecting teams 83, 85-6
    resource, use of, 67-8
    schools of, 11
    skills 115, 121-3, 129-31, 152-3
    sponsorship 140-1
    stool, 51
    strategic 23
    strategy 25, 30-1, 33-43, 67, 102, 181
    strategy workshop 36-40
    supervision, definition of, 156
    suppliers 133-4
    syndicate learning 83-5
    team 91-8
    transformational 87, 115, 153-4
    whole-system 4
Coaching culture 21-32
    artefacts 22
    behaviours 22
    developmental stages of, 22-5
    emotional ground 22
    mindsets 22
    motivational roots 22
    Seven Step Model of creating, 27-32
Coaching Foundation Course (CFC) 73
Coaching service
    annual review 70, 163
    collaboration 71-2
    internal 140
    review of, 157-8
    structure of, 24-7
Coaching strategy 25-6
    appreciative inquiry 37-8
    fishbone strategy building 38
    review 43
    three pillars of, 25-7
    workshop 36-40
Cogntive frame of reference 153
Collaborative working 42
Communication skills 73, 147
Community of practice 27
Complete value chain 147-8
Complex-adaptive organisations 80-1
Confidentiality 55, 58, 59, 61
    Harvesting the learning 99-103
        coaching offering 102
        coaching process 101
        coaching style for managers 102
        communication 102
        development of coaches 101
        emerging themes 100
        performance management 102
        supervision 102
        utilization of coaches 101
Conflict of interest 55

Consultation 40
Continuous personal and professional development (CPPD) 154–5
  supervision, and 69–70
  retention of internal coaches, and 142
Continuing professional development (CPD) 9, 50, 57–8, 101, 154–5
Contracting
  coaching conversation purpose and objectives of, 117
  customer 128
  meeting 56
  three-way process 55–7, 99, 162, 180
  four-way process 56–7, 99
  in workshop 97
Conversations 177
  generative dialogue 177–9
Core skills and capabilities 26
  active listening 118
  agreement, establishment of, 65
  assessment for internal coaches 66–7
  analytical skills 73
  building relationships 73
  CLEAR Model 117–18
  coach criteria 50–1
  coaching presence 65
  communcation skills 65, 73
  emotional intelligence 13
  establishing trust 65
  ethical guidelines and standards 65
  intervention 73
  International Coaching Federation competencies 65–6
  managing progress 66
  personal development 155
  planning and goal setting 66
  recruitment, necessary for, 65
  self-awareness 73
  'shift in the room' 153
  'shifting the meaning scheme' 153
CPPD see Continuous personal and professional development
Crisis intervention 60
Crosse, Elizabeth 142
Culture
  change 114, 143–7
  change plan 42
  definitions of, 35
  five levels of, 22, 35–6
  framework, coaching 28–32
  leadership and team 144–7

Customer
  relationship with, 148
  satisfaction 180
  service 105

'Dangerous derailers' 105–6
Darwin, Charles 126
Delta Air Lines 129
Denial patterns 106
Department of Justice 142
Development
  conversations 110–11
  feedback 111
  reviews 39, 49
  long-term 110
Developmental inputs 169
Dialogue
  generative 177–8
Dolan, Maxine 23
Drucker, Peter 35
Dyke, Greg 72, 106

Electricity Supply Board (Ireland) 70, 163
  case study 101–3
EMCC see European Mentoring and Coaching Council
Emotional ground 22
Emotional intelligence (EQ) 13
Emotional patterns 154
Employee
  engagement 105
  performance and team dynamics 145–7
Engagement
  Four levels of, 82, 118–19
  Torbet styles of, 118–19
Enron 178
Environment 126
Ernst & Young
  case study, 34, 86–7
  coaching resource, 68
  Coaching White Paper 34
  leadership programme 86–7
Ethical
  boundaries 55
  codes of practice 126
  dilemma 53
  maturity 154
European Commission 85
European Mentoring and Coaching Council (EMCC) 50, 65, 158
  training, accreditation of, 67, 73

Evaluation
  balanced scorecards 165
  of coaching culture and supervision, 160–8
  criteria 55
  external audit 163–4
  key performance indicators (KPIs) 164
  stakeholder feedback 167–8
Evolution 126
Executive coaching 49–51
External coaches 6–7, 23
  advantages of, 62
  panel of, 47–59
  pool of, 48
  resource 48–59
  selection process, 54, 59

Facilitation, by consultant, 100
Facilitator 98
FCO *see* UK Foreign and Commonwealth Office
Feedback
  360-degree, 55, 76, 99, 112, 121–2, 164–5
  CORBS, 119
  data analysis 167–8
  descriptor analysis 164
  evaluation, as part of, 161–2
  instruments of, 55
  and organizational learning 70
  process 55
  written 58
Fields, Mark 34
Firo-B 55
Fishbone strategy building 38–40
Fisher, R. and Ury, W. 134
Ford Motor Company 34
Foundational pillar 24–7, 33
Four domains of learning 13–14
Four levels of engagement 82, 91, 118, 153–4
Framework
  coaching skills 116
  coaching strategy 28–32
  for creating a coaching culture, 28–32
  leadership 82
  of relational value change, 147–51
  for shortlist of applicants, 51–2
FTSE 100 Cross-Company Mentoring Programme 63–4

Gender awareness programmes 107
General Electric 83
Ghandi, Mahatma 88

Global economic crisis 2008–10 16

Harvard Business Review
  research report 16
Hawkins, Peter 2, 8, 13, 16, 35, 50, 56, 84, 92, 93, 154, 155, 168, 179
Hawkins, P. and Chesterman, D. 155
Hawkins, P. and Schwenk, G. 50, 69, 155
Hawkins, P. and Shohet, R. 129, 159
Hawkins, P. and Smith, N. 2, 13, 27, 35, 50, 56, 82, 115, 117, 118, 119, 152, 156, 168
Hawkins, P. and Wright, A. 79, 86
Head of coaching 5
Health coaching 5–6, 131–2
Heffernan, M. 178–9
Henley Business School
  learning syndicates 83–4
  senior management training 83–4
High performance culture 112
High-performing leadership teams 2, 91–98
  clarifying 94
  co-creating 94
  commissioning 93
  connecting 94
  core learning 94
  five disciplines of 93–6
  team performance 92–3
Högberg, Britt-Marie 144
Holland, Mary 85
HSBC Holdings plc (HSBC) 51, 68
Human Resources (HR)
  coaching as an HR initiative 40–1, 141
  coaching development plan, role in, 23, 141
  coaching policy and guidelines 49–56
  coaching strategy 33
  director, challenges of 4–5
  'harvesting the learning' 99–100
  managing performance 15, 109–11, 166
  matching coach and client 68
  processes and strategy 104, 166
  recruiting coaches 65
  reward measures 111–12
Huthwaite 128–9

Individual objectives *see* personal objectives
Institute for Employment Studies 163
Institute of Leadership and Management 61
  coaching qualification 122
  training, accreditation of, 67, 142

Institutional sexism 107
Internal coaches 6, 62–4
  advantages of, 62
  retention of, 142
Internal coaching community 61, 64–71,
  continuous personal and professional
    development 69–70
  evaluation and feedback process on,
    163–4
  matching client and coach 68–9
  planning 64
  recruitment 65
  supervision 69–71
  training and development 67, 72–8
Internal facilitators 98–9
Internal mentors 62–4
International Coach Federation (ICF) 50, 65
  2007 survey 11
  accreditation 73
  key coach capabilities, capacities,
    competencies 65–6
Investor coaching 132–3

Japan Airlines 129

Key coaching relationships 100
Knights, A. and Poppleton, A. 23–4
Knowledge management strategy 34
Key Performance Indicators (KPIs) 102,
  109–12, 165
KPMG 65
Kramer, Michael 126–7

Lambert, Liz 130–1
Leader
  adaptive 80
  coaching style, key attributes of, 81–2
  'four levels of engagement' 82
  heroic 80
Leadership
  challenges 81
  coaching skills 140
  coaching style 81
  collective 1, 180
  conference 98–9
  culture 79, 144–7
  development 1, 13–14, 38, 76
  development programmes 83–6, 180
  facilitator style of, 122
  high-performing teams 93–6
  programmes 82

strategy 42, 166
studies 80
Lean Process and Design 148
Learning
and continuous improvement, 105
cycles 157
and development, 13–14
'harvesting the learning' 99–100
as mode of teaching, 111
Legal Services Commission 142
Lehman Brothers 178
Lincoln, Shaun 156
Line manager 72–3, 115
Lived brand 12, 136

Macann, Liz 64, 72, 74
McCarthy, Tom, 175
McDowell, Dr Andrew 132
Management
  coaching, as style of, 166–7
  group 26
  performance 176
  training 140
Manager
  as coach, 7, 115
  CIPD research 115–16
  coaching characteristics 115–16
  coaching skills 72–3, 116–20
  evaluation of, 163–4
  selection process 107
Marshall, Colin 82
Masters of Business Administration (MBA)
  50
Maxwell, Alison 60–1
Mentor
  differences between coach and, 63
  internal 62–4
Medica 131
Mergers and acquisitions 34
Milner, Dr Brigid 164
Mindsets 22, 82, 100, 177
Motivational roots 22, 100
Myer-Briggs 55

National Health Service 69, 132
National Health Service North West
  Leadership Academy 72
National Professional Qualification in
  Headship 57
National Training Award 122
Newman, Dr Penny 132

NHS Institute for Innovation and
    Improvement 51, 52, 58, 69, 157
Nippon Airways 129
Non-performance management 107
North West Employers 72
    Chief Executive coaching programme 136

Obolensky, N. 80
Outsource 15
Organizational
    aspirations 37
    behaviour 50
    core values 54
    culture 100
    culture change 25, 36, 79, 144–51, 176
    development 8, 41, 100, 151
    development plan 25
    emotions 100
    goals 167
    learning 13–15, 59, 70
    mindsets 100
    mission, 41, 54, 176
    motivational roots 100
    objectives 37, 176
    patterns of behaviour 100
    strategy 54, 176
Organization
complex-adaptive 80–1
Oshry, B. 90
Oxfam case study 130–1

Panel of executive coaches 47–59
Patient, coaching of, 131–2
Partner organizations 133–4
Pedler, M. 13, 83–4
Performance
    appraisals 39
    improvement 105
    management 176
Personal objectives
    360-degree feedback 112
    balanced scorecard 108
    key performance indicators 112
    performance indicators 109
        task outputs 109
        outcome objectives 109
    reward, linking to, 111
Personality structures, narcissistic 106
Perspectives
    external 37
    internal 37

Pilot 40
    study 57
Pincheta, Barbara 156
Porsgaard, Rüddi 144
Porter, Michael 126–7
Pricewaterhouse Coopers 65, 156
Prince of Wales Trust 135–6
Professional capability 105
Professional services firms 63, 135
Project Phoenix (Sweden) 140, 144–7
Psychometric instruments 55
Public sector partnerships 133

Qualitative studies 77
Quantas 129

Rackham, Neil 128
Regulator, engagement with, 134–5
Relational capacity 154
Relational value chain 9, 13, 36, 147–51
Relationship
    effective empathetic 90–1
    skills 42
    staff, 145–7
Research
    on coaching 171–4, 179
    Hawkins' model of coaching research 173
    Leedham's model of coaching
        research 173
    methodology 169–71
Revans, Reg 83
Return on Investment (ROI) 3, 10, 98, 161,
        168–71
    definition of, 170
Royal Navy
    case study
    CLEAR model of coaching, adaption of
        117–19
Royal Society for the Encouragement of Arts,
        Manufactures and Commerce
        (RSA) 125
Ryde, Judy 107

Sceptics 106
Scott, Lynn 72
Selection
    of coaches, 51, 106–7
    open book joint selection 55
    open book self-selection 55
Self-awareness 73
Service users 129–31

INDEX

Seven Step Model of Creating a Coaching Culture 27–32, 139–40
   sequence of, 139–40
Shared learning group 74, 77
Shared value 126
Sherpa Executive Coaching 170
Six Sigma 148
Southern Railway
   case study 121–3
SPIN selling approach 128–9
Sponsorship 140–1
Staff
   absenteeism 166
   development 107
   engagement 122–3
   retention of, 141–2
   salutogenic approach to development of, 144–7
   satisfaction survey 166–7
   volunteer 135–6
Stakeholder
   community 135–6
   engagement 9
   group 37
   'lived brand' 136, 148–51
   perceptions 148
   relationships 125–7, 148–51
   shared value 126–7, 172–3
Steering group 26
Strandska 144
Supervision 155–9
   coaching, definition of, 156
   good practice 69
   hours 69
   importance of, 159
   of managers, 157
   trios 100
Sustainability 80, 126
Systemic team coaching 93, 180
   definition of, 93

Teacher Support Network 155
Teaching 111
Team
   development 93
   dynamics 145
   leadership 92
   performance evaluation 164–5
   sales 128–9, 168
Team coaching 91–98
   building, definition of 93
   coaching style meeting 97–8, 120–121
   development, definition of 93
   development, of 164–5
   facilitation, definition of 93
   high performing teams 91–98
   systemic, definition of 93, 180
   team process consultancy 93
Tesco 23
Thames Valley Police Force 82
Thomson, Peninah, 63
Thomson Reuters Executive Coaching Services 49
Tolstoy, L.N. 80
Torbert, W. 82, 118, 153
Total Quality Management 148
Toyota 148
Training
   accreditation of, 67
   courses 7
Transformational coaching 87, 153–4

UK Department of Work and Pensions
   case study 104
UK Foreign and Commonwealth Office
   case study 41–42
   coaching strategy 41–2, 165, 168
   definition of coaching 42
Unipart 148
United Airlines 129

Welch, Jack 83
West Midland Local Government Association 71
Whitmore, Sir John
Wright, Andrew 86

Xerox 129

Yeovil District Hospital Foundation Trust
   case study 96–7